Cloud of Expectation

Book One: The **In America** series

Mike Westphal

Library of Congress Control Number:		2016905942
ISBN:	Hardcover	978-1-5144-8317-6
	Softcover	978-1-5144-8316-9
	eBook	978-1-5144-8315-2

Print information available on the last page.

Rev. date: 05/20/2016

To order additional copies of this book, contact:
Xlibris
1-888-795-4274
www.Xlibris.com
Orders@Xlibris.com
738613

CONTENTS

1: Neighborhood & Town

OUR TOWN

To children
the past is vague
--- all conjecture.

All we knew was, some things --- wisps, intentions
clay & sawdust
had drawn together and solidified
into brick and wood siding
and streets, with globes of light at the curb.
Men and their labors had been drawn toward
some hidden ideal, and had settled at last
into a most satisfying town.
Shops and residences
were surrounded by
a green pleated countryside
thick forested hills, draining to
lakes and rivers in the lowlands.

Giant old trees overhung the streets,
a ballfield adjoined the churchyard
while, on every block, ladies sat on their front porches
murmuring greetings to
the kids who ran or tumbled by in their celebrations
and to the old men who hobbled along
grinning their ancient knowledge
now a benevolence.

To me, it was perfect, I thought
the ghost of the Ideal or the hidden Tao
governed it all.

So I became an enthusiast for Things As They Were.

The sun rose, casting long shadows
across the streets and upon the
walls of the houses opposite --- a stark new light.

Bacon was peeled and laid sizzling in the pan. Tables were set.
Children were wakened from their beds.
The grownups had agreed to bind them over to the schools, but
vacations were long, and weekends . . . yes . . . weekends . . .

In the shops and the warehouses, men slid long keys into padlocks
and rolled back the doors.

The workday had begun, but we knew nothing of the furnace
the forklift or the framing hammer
the iron wheels of the boxcars
or the red light at the crossing, the harsh shading of the loading-dock
the refrigerated trucks
lanterns at 5 AM, tires grinding on the gravel
we did not know of the years of
careful paycheck calculation:
how much to pay and what to postpone.
We knew only that a calm world
had been devised, a pleasant setting
for our wide-eyed romp.

A luminous cloud of expectation surrounded us
as we jumped off the steps
each day
and entered a new world.

The ladies who sat on the front porches
wore long, light dresses, spotted with dots or prints of flowers
and murmured to one another in low wavering voices:
a burble of memory, regret, resignation and, sometimes,
of ease and passing pleasure in the moment.
They might call you over
to question you.
They seemed to know all about your ancestry
and to savor the moments
they could get you to pause and speak.
They seemed to consider, as they took your measure
what you would become, and how you'd fit into
the world they were handing over to you
a world still partly theirs
the world they'd have to relinquish.

I looked into their questioning eyes, and then
a light breeze called me
to run on down the street.

The old men who'd served their time
as plumbers, upholsterers, countermen, sheet-metal workers
(whose injuries had returned to bedevil them
because the healings had frayed)
left their homes daily, and sauntered down the block
to the church hall, where they played poker, blackjack
checkers, even chess
and argued the deeds of the day, with
a tall gold beer at their left hand.

Truly a Papist den of iniquity: drinking, gambling, and
the smell of hops and old leather.

On the sidewalk, one of them might walk with me
to the churchyard, or its clubhouse-basement.

Aboveground, I would
whack a ball into the backstop netting
or, seeking my grandfather, have a look downstairs.

Dimness, and a grumble of voices
and odors ancient and familiar.
Descending, I found an oversized chair
and sat, watching the cards fly
listening to the rumble
and savoring the company of men.

One day the neighborhood Baptist --- not a bad fellow, really ---
came down to the church hall to complain
about a car parked in front of his house.
As he entered the door, the six o'clock bells rung for the Angelus
and the old men rose from their chairs and dropped to their knees
and began mumbling in Latin.

He didn't know what the hell was going on.

The brown people could be seen at the edge of things
cutting wood, taking in washing, trimming hedge,
stacking feed sacks, riding the bus (usually at the back),
sweating deep in the kitchen (at the restaurant)
and patching up tires at the garage.
Between exertions, they settled back on the feed bags,
or on the brick wall, and then,
at their moments of rest, seemed to draw their breath
from a deep reservoir of ease, as a man might draw from a cigarette,
and to share in some silent low communion,
their voices like bassoons and flutes
in muted conversation, woodwinds in call-and-response.
On the bus, they filled the air with a hovering presence, near to
                                        tangible ---
two ladies in amused conversation might provoke a nod of agreement
from several sundry stragglers, a clearing of throat here, a roll of eye and
jiggle of knuckles there. "I know that's so."

        To a child, this was remarkable, because each white bus-rider sat
alone in his cell, wrapped in the intractable.

Then, nothing more than children, our brains were scarred
by the TV images
of shouting mobs determined to keep them out of the schools.
I DIDN'T KNOW, my brain said.

My father had been quite a sport in his younger day
playing baseball at the churchyard
till the heat broke and evening fell
and bats fluttered overhead
and the cricket- and frog-voices came out and the
streetlamps flared on like creamy moons.
Under the guidance of the old men at the church hall
he'd learned to play poker and begun to drink beer; and,
when he went to work at the tire warehouse, he learned to shoot dice
with the brown boys who were his workmates.

He and my aunt say that in the neighborhoods they knew, there was
no racial animosity, that the children lived in a prelapsarian Eden
of innocence. All of them ran after the ice-wagon, played tricks on
the electric streetcar, and called each other the impolite names until
adulthood intervened. It was neither Mississippi with its gun-toting
terrorism --- keeping 'em in place --- nor New York with its violent
ethnic warfare of nationalities. It was Arkansas.

My father and his workmates opened the warehouse on Friday and
Saturday nights and chained it shut from the inside. The owners knew
nothing. Crouched down in a circle, they brought out the white cubes
and the dimes and the quarters.

Their cries were like the shouts at each pitch at a baseball game. A man
riding a hot streak threw his magic on the dice with a boasting, shoulder-
swinging sound; when he won, he exclaimed; when he lost he felt he'd
been struck. Apparently bad attitude was not a problem, for Stagger
Lee never returned to shoot Billy, or I think --- I believe --- my father
would have told me about it.

The Germans had planted their communities across Arkansas, and named them for places half a world away; in the cities, they gathered in tight neighborhoods and so kept the ways and language of the old country while adapting to the opportunities of the new. The people on my father's side were German --- one from a pair of brothers who emigrated in the 1840's --- they kept their papers showing they were legally released by their landholder and were not runaways. Apparently a decayed feudalism had interfaced with the new bureaucracy to create certificates of inequality. Another came over in the 1870's, to escape conscription, and worked his way inland as an ox-cart driver, finally buying his own team and wagon in Arkansas, where he made short hauls, probably catching his business from the German communities that liked to bargain with their own. In one of these he found the girl he was to marry, and he settled with her in her hometown of Stuttgart.

The Germans brought with them the ways and skills of small tradesmen: butchers and bakers and candlestick makers. And they brought the tradition of brewing. Beer was their relaxation after work, and home brewing a popular art, especially during Prohibition. Beer was woven into the fabric of their life, while hard liquor was not, unlike, perhaps, the Irish, whose drinking was so often destructive. In the North, Germans looked to Milwaukee as their capital; in the South, both before and after Prohibition, they looked to St. Louis, with its Anheuser-Busch brewery. I do remember the old men always talking about St. Louis.

The new generation embraced the American game of baseball, and when St. Louis fielded a pro team, the Germans made it 'theirs'. Listening to the Cardinals on the radio became the weekend recreation of the late 1920's. The Cardinals cultivated a handful of farm teams, and these circulated through the area's venues, playing each other or whatever teams the locals could muster. My father and his best friend sold refreshments at our local field, running up and down the stands and watching the games while picking up boy-sized pockets of silver.

Each house spread
its outstretched wings
and filled a greater spiritual space
than its actual wooden dimensions.
Each life, inside,
had grown like the trunk of a grapevine
on the arbor of marriage.

Little sprigs sought the sun.

During the Depression, my father said,
people sometimes could not make their payments
and the house was in danger of foreclosure.
Then, word went around the neighborhood
and a house party was announced.
Ground beef was fried and drained, for
the German-Americans had taken to Mexican food
as an easy dinner for hard times.
Tomatoes and lettuce were chopped, cheese grated, and
taco shells stuffed.
Everyone came and brought a dollar or two
for the pleasure of a social evening.
Someone brought an accordion, and often as not
a piano saw use in the parlor. The Germans
made as merry with beer and song as their dignity would allow,
                                                 while

children crawled around their feet or sat under the table.
When the evening was over, the house payment was there.

THE PARISH CHURCH

Blocky and Romanesque,
it governed the neighborhood like a small city hall,
collecting the besieged Catholics
and bulwarking them against
surly mob growlings
and xenophobic suspicions
from outsiders.

The pastor, a cigar-puffing bulldog of a man
answered the needs of his people:
heard their secret confidences
and their troubles
and arranged for help
as surely as the mythic Don Corleone
had heard petitions and administered justice
in his small office.

Every day the bells swung ---
heavy brass bells
and the children at their checkered oilcloth tabletops
morning eggs over easy, chicken in the evening
were forcibly reminded of celestial governance.

Bong! Bong!

On Sundays, the good folk filed down the sidewalks
to fulfill their sacred duty:
fine-feathered hens with little chicks at their heels
sober burghers nodding hellos
the elderly clinging to their arms.

When at last Mass was over and the doors swung wide
and the bells clanged out a celebration
the folk stood blinking in the sunlight
then gingerly let themselves down the steps

to renew their vows of neighborliness, so to speak, but
the afternoon ahead was wide open, and
Sunday dinner and radio baseball were on every mind.

Now the bells' clappers struck the chains from the children,
free to run as the breeze carried them
out of the living-rooms and out of doors and down the sidewalks
leaving the adults and their big-bodied sloth behind.

Four times a day the secular pipes tooted, the factory whistles
blowing at eight, noon, one o'clock and five
reminding kids of great airy spaces
steam calliopes and passing trains
calling to mind adventures and open skies
when actually, they presaged just the opposite:
confinement, iron machinery, a screeching planer, or a screw gun
wielded in a huge dark room
where men rendered to Caesar what Caesar asked.

Carnegie had endowed a library
walled it in stone, strengthened it with pillars, put in a wide staircase
and set it back from the street
in the cool shaded space beneath the oaks
and placed a bicycle rack to one side.

A causeway of aged concrete led to the swinging doors
and to the treasures racked inside
or heaped up on the moving carts ---
books about dinosaurs
lizards
big hard-shelled beetles
caves
Moomins
odd beasts of the tropics
extraterrestrial adventures of the future
and the heroic men of yesteryear
whose droopy mustaches hid mouths firm with resolve.

To emerge from its tomblike hush
to the world outside
was to pass from wide-ranging mind
to life-savoring body
and be grateful for both.

The brightness of the day
broke the reading trance, while
playful air bathed our pores
and welcomed us back.

To unrack the bicycle and pedal it on down the street
rising, to pump harder
was to sport like a muscular dolphin
while trailing clouds of delicious mind fizz

On other days we would return to tap the casks
inside, and sample the many flavored distillations.

The pulp world of detective magazines and western magazines and adventure magazines filled the newsstands, but my father was never one for reading while life was fresh. He learned to hunt young, and he learned to fish when my grandfather took him out to the lake, renting a boat to row half a mile to the good spots.

My grandfather had done his duty in life and now in the open days of retirement was somewhat lost. Inactivity did not suit him. His hands longed for tools. Orphaned early, in the 1890's, he was taken in by relatives, who taught him the butcher's trade; by then he'd become a quiet boy, more interested in the thicket and the wild creatures he found when he went exploring down by the river. With the help of books, he'd learned the names of every flower, vine, shrub and tree; the animals' names were common knowledge. When I was small, he gave me a coloring book with the animals in line drawings, and he showed me how to color their coats.

And when school was out, he and my father took me to the lake to fish.

During summers, the lake was a living metaphor for eternity --- still, shimmering --- with wavelets slapping the shore and dragonflies hovering over the docks, all reached by a winding dirt road through the mountains. We would park the car in the grass and extract the poles --- bamboo and fiberglass --- and walk to the ancient boat rental, where old men waited in the shade beneath a corrugated tin roof, with cold soda pop and nightcrawlers for sale. Money passed over and words exchanged --- my father hearty, the old men cryptic as hounds --- I carried the bait bucket down the weathered steps and swung it into the boat, minding my balance. My grandfather, as always, wore his bib overalls and long johns.

"Doin' alright, Dad?" My father to his.

"Yeh, Bud, yeh."

We slipped into the seats and my father dipped the oars and the boat surged forward. Loosed from the dock, we found ourselves in a world of fluid mechanics where the creatures of water and air moved with a greater ease than ourselves. We might see silvery bass rise to the surface to snap and plunge down, leaving the water disturbed, while lazy-winged birds drifted overhead and a curious dragonfly followed to keep us company. Below, in the transparent depths, mid-sized bluegill would zig, pause, and zag, while smaller shyer fish hid among the lily pads, emerging in quick darting schools to cross a short & unsecured expanse. A waterlogged tree might float in the deeps, with ruined branch beckoning like Ahab's dead arm; turtles rested on its wet back, sunning, heaving off or climbing back on. When we folded the oars and came to rest, the brown-green water lapped at the sides of the boat, the sun god looked down, the silence was immense, and the presence of life in the air was palpable. I put my hand in the water; it was warm.

We baited the hooks and dropped our lines in the water. The older men had explained to me that spearing earthworms and minnows did not hurt them, and I believed them. As we settled back in our seats, the boat might continue to rock, driven by the low swells although no wind seemed to move. As I looked out across the immensities and breathed in the mud-scented air, I could fall into the sun-dazzled trance of forever. For me, the fishing was almost superfluous; the lake itself was enough.

Soon enough, my meditations would be interrupted when the cork jiggled and the line telegraphed me a message.

At the age of fourteen, my father had acquired a desire for a boat with an outboard motor, and somehow, through his contacts, he found both; he always had a job and during Depression time people were willing to sell what they did not need. Then, he and his friend would cruise up and down the river, seeking the best fishing spots and keeping the boat tied up at a secret location. One day they arrived at their hidden spot and the boat was no longer there. They had their suspicions.

Down the water a bit was a riverbank community of hard-timers, where the homeless and the jobless mixed with the criminal and itinerant. My father and his friend did a nighttime reconnaissance of the settlement and discovered his boat. Under the cover of darkness, they cut it free and, holding to its side with one hand and swimming with the other, they drifted with the current till they were far away enough to climb in and start up the motor.

After that, they hid it much better, under a thick brace of branches, and the thieves made no second attempt.

My father and the internal combustion engine had a rocky history. For him it was a fatal attraction, an affair with a wild unpredictable woman he could not leave alone, and it brought him more pain and sorrow than it was worth. The outboard motor was only the beginning, a puppy love that ended well, so it seduced him into riskier and more dangerous entanglements.

One evening he returned to the tire warehouse after Christmas shopping on foot. One of his luckier workmates owned a car. "Say Ralph," he called, "let me take your car to drop off these presents." Ralph and his friends were lounging on the tires, having a beer after the day's work. "Ralph, my friend," said Eugene, seated nearby, "I go with him, he can drop me off at my girlfriend's." Ralph was as agreeable as a man should be under those circumstances. He handed the keys over to my father.

A light rain had begun to fall.

"That little old gal, she waiting on me tonight."

My father expressed his enthusiasm, insofar as his Catholic upbringing would allow.

"Now which way are we gonna go?" he asked, after they had pulled away. Eugene gave him a set of directions he could not follow. "Here," said Gene, "Lemme get us there." They swapped places.

Gene took the wheel and turned down a residential street. Rain had begun to spatter the windshield. He was driving a little too fast, because the beer in him had clouded his judgment and the thought of his girlfriend was drawing him on. He flicked on the wipers, hit a curb, flipped over and skidded on down the street on the roof, spinning, coming to rest ten feet off the paving when they struck a tree in a lady's front yard. The two boys crawled out, unhurt. Shaken, Eugene regained his senses.

"They gon' send me to jail for this, I been drinkin and drivin," he moaned. He sat crouched up under a great fern, head cradled in his arms, the darkness of consequences crashing in on him.

My father could not stand to see his workmate in despair. "I'll say I was driving, Gene," he said. "I'm sober, and I got no record."

"Oh, look at my garden!" wailed the lady, on the porch.

And that was how it worked out.

Although I may have presented Eugene in comic fashion --- deservedly so --- he and my father were the two best dice players in the warehouse, for neither one believed in hunches or magic. They both knew the odds --- 6-5, 6-4, 6-3, 6-2, and 6-1 --- and bet against the shooter when they could get a sweeter deal than the math allowed, which was always. Ralph's car was repaired, on credit, and in less than a year the two boys had paid the shop for all damages.

My father's subsequent history with the internal combustion engine will go untold. There was irresponsibility; there were injuries --- he almost lost his left forearm, and had to argue forcefully with the doctors to be allowed to keep it.

Insects teemed
beneath every leaf and stone.
I studied
their veined wings, their horny shells
their bodies, enigmatic and odd
like the heraldic beasts on medieval coats of arms
tiny hard black eyes
connected to limited nervous systems
their graven pupae, like Egyptian sarcophagi
in which they lay, slowly transformed
and from which they emerged
one bright day
legs a-splay, dragging wings behind
with all the wet coloring of morning.

The rhinoceros beetle --- what a brute!
His slimmer cousin, an Ichabod Crane
nerdy and brown and nondescript;
the ant-lions that waited concealed
at the bottom of their sandy holes
whom I teased into impatience with my fake straw-slides
angry little beasts, they tossed plumes of dust
and sometimes I could lift one out, his enormous jaws
clamped on my grass-blade;
walking-sticks, my favorites, slow and careful
their circumspect tread showing all the wisdom
of a hundred million years;
the June-beetle, whose gold and green carapace
seemed to capture all the high promise, the endless winding pathway
of grade-school summer.

Everything that wriggled and sought to escape me
--- these were my friends.

The stars spilled like sugar across the night, and
the air was warm and salty as any bloodstream:
evergreen resin and loamy leaf-rot in my nose
a spicy mix stirred by God's spoon.

Air trailed across my flesh,
veils of tease and temptation.

I inspected an insect on a twig, then
lay back in the grass
waiting to be born to the universe.

Frogs shrilled, and bats flapped
and slowly the moon went down.
The trees whispered, but
soon I began to itch.

Well, maybe another night
the Great Mystery will be revealed to me.
Night belonged to the Great Mystery, and
the Mystery and I had a date --- no doubt about it.

In his adulthood, my grandfather gave up butchering and took up sheet-metal work, using nippers and hammers and torches to customize the rolled sheets for the particular job. When the Depression came, he found work on the projects Washington created for Arkansas --- roofs for schools, auxiliary equipment for dam construction --- and so kept his family in food and shelter. Had Roosevelt not been so committed to the solvency of the working man, he and his family would have lost all. Traditional economic dogma would've dictated that he go unemployed, naked to the world, at the beck and call of men whose purses were closed tight until they saw profit could be made once again. As it was, he had the means to take in a flock of relatives who were not so fortunate.

Uncle John was one of these. He had been a fireman in his younger day; I have a photograph of him and his mates lined up by the fire horse. He looks husky and affable. But he put himself at the mercy of fortune, seeking better pay as a coal miner --- a reasonable thing to do at the time --- and when the system broke down he was laid off and the union could not save him or his job. Only his brother could help.

The government jobs gave my grandfather a little pocket money, and with this he was able to take advantage of the knock-down rents of the time and open a little garage. Automobile radiators were always developing leaks, and he had the tools and the know-how. Thus did stimulus money from Washington work its magic.

My father and his brother learned the basics of auto mechanics on the oil-stained floor of the family garage.

THE MINES

Forty miles from town were the coal mines, where men descended hundreds of feet in elevator cages for ten- and twelve-hour shifts. Crouched down under a five-foot ceiling, they drilled and blasted and loaded the rail-carts and came up black and lung-crusted and ready for bath and bed, or dinner at the family table, or liquor and roistering in the hell-mills by the river.

Riding back from town, some of the men would shoot down the shafts to hear the bullets ricochet off the walls for a thousand feet.

Mines could be excavated on the slope or on the straight perpendicular. A slope mine needed no elevator, but both types used mules to pull the loaded rail cars. In the dank deep tunnels, there was little a man could do to escape a methane explosion or a dust explosion or a flash fire. Hearing the rumble coming his way, he might hide behind a rock pillar and hope not to be burned to death. If there was standing water nearby, he might fling himself into it. Afterwards, if he survived, he had to breathe air already stripped of oxygen by the combustion, and saturated with carbon monoxide. Suffocation was the usual fate of the immediate survivors.

After a disaster --- a cave-in or explosion --- men noticed that the owners were more concerned about the mules lost than the men. Men were a renewable resource --- more were waiting in line --- while the new mules had to be paid for.

While John L. Lewis was fighting for recognition of the United Mine Workers Union --- and giving the miners new backbone as he did --- strikes broke out in the coalfields like strings of firecrackers. Miners meant to shut down production so the owners tried to truck in new workers to break the unions. Men armed themselves and guarded the roads to the mines. Gunbattles broke out. A whole history of the United States is hidden here through educational neglect and cinematic disinterest. An armed population was not resisting a theoretical tyrannical government, as current right-wing fantasy projects --- they were fighting the masters of capital, the 'job creators', to whom today we are told to sacrifice everything --- wages, future, tax revenue --- turn ourselves into trembling supplicants so that they do not fold our jobs and go elsewhere.

Families that had to live with constant fear and worry were held together by ties beyond what we now recognize. One wife thought she heard her husband call for help, so she stepped outside, but he was nowhere in sight. Half a minute later the sirens went off. There had been an explosion three hundred feet under the ground. Another, a twelve-year-old boy, lay dreaming he heard taps being played. He awoke and, finding his father had not come home, feared the worst and ran to the mine entrance, where he was told his father had been killed.

On a lighter note --- if there can be one after that --- my father went down in the mines once. He had a buddy who offered to show him around. They rode the elevator down, and as they walked along the tunnel his friend bumped against some overhanging obstacle, knocked his helmet off and their carbide lamp went out. The two were left in total darkness. They began to feel their way around. "Let me find something to strike a match against," said his friend, and after a minute he found some rough wood. The match flared, and my father saw he had struck the match against a box of dynamite.

"Let's get out of here right now," my dad said, and it is fortunate that they did, or you might not be reading this.

In the late 1930's my father and his friends were full-grown, but the nation's recovery had been too slow. Much of the economy crawled along on relief, subsistence, help from friends, and credit from shopkeepers. The near-men of the neighborhood, bursting with energy and new needs, were ready to take on a man's role, but could find little or nothing that would satisfy them. They wanted green in their hands; they wanted an open door to life. So boredom and dissatisfaction ruled them.

Sometimes they would pool their money and buy a pitcher of beer at a small bar just outside the neighborhood and wait for the nurses to get off their shift. A nickel would set the juke-box going, and they would dance with one and then another of the nurses, who were undoubtedly paid better than they were.

There had to be a better way.

Collectively, the boys came to a slow decision: they would all join the Army. When they had served their time, the economy would be better, and good jobs would be waiting for them. In two years, they'd be back.

It was to have been a great new adventure, like a hunting trip or an out-of-town ball game. They would see the world and make new friends. But then one Sunday, all along the West coast, from California to Alaska, sirens screamed and guys piled out of the mess halls & the barracks, found their guns & slapped on their helmets. There would be no play-acting this time.

The war was here for real, but most of the Arkansas guys had already been sent to Alaska --- though a few were eventually sent to Europe. Japanese planes bombed Dutch Harbor, in Alaska --- the only part of the North American mainland to be hit --- and Japanese troops landed on two of the Aleutian Islands, where they starved, froze, fought with miserable dedication, and held on to one island for a month before evacuating in the dead of night --- the strategic gain was too small and resupply, in the stormy ice-seas, was a nightmare. They were needed elsewhere, and soon the Japanese invasion of Alaska faded from memory, crowded out by the spectacular battles of the Pacific and the Allied invasion of Europe. Left out of the schoolbooks, it is now a forgotten sideshow, a curiosity remembered chiefly in Arkansas.

But the War was a big story, and we sure can't tell it here.

"Your dad had a way with people," my mother told me. "He was everything I wasn't. I was scared of everybody."

As I got older I watched his method. Although 'hearty' was a word that could be applied, he wasn't a backslapper. Instead, he would go up to strangers and intrude --- hail them, surprise them --- get past their guard to get them to laughing. Then, in the loose swirl that followed, he would jab, pat, use his arms or hands to enlarge upon the temporary intimacy. He seemed to enjoy himself this way.

In the army, he had received promotion after promotion because his officers saw him as a man the other men would follow without resentment. Or, that was half the story. The other half was, so long as he was allowed his gambling and his hunting, he would buckle down and do the work. He had a kind of an engineer's practical intelligence about how to do things.

The last time I went back to Arkansas, he was ninety-plus, and we walked across our acres to where some young brown men were digging a fence line along a neighbor's property. Suddenly, there went the jokes and the jabs. He was mixing it up with them, and their smiles, a bit indulgent at first for this ninety-year-old who had come up out of nowhere, were full-hearted after he had got them going. He was back in the tire warehouse again.

The old neighborhood broke apart after the War, its children grown & blown like seed-fluff all over town by new marriages and easy credit and the homebuilding boom. Some remained behind to perpetuate what was left of the old German-inflected ville, just in time for me to fall under its influence and take it as my own. Among the several parts of town I knew this was my favorite, more so after I reached high school and met the boys who had come up in the same area.

"This is where I should have grown up," I told my father, and he took it as I meant it --- as an affirmation, a small benediction. "Well," he said, "that makes me feel real good."

Over the years I've always scribbled away, using the short-line form, and a number of these pieces, these 'poems' -- so-called, though they neither rhyme nor scan --- have to do with the old neighborhood --- what wannabe writer does not return to this well --- and as I read them over I am struck by how 'positive' they are, for they detail a child's open-faced entry into the world. The sad or limiting facts of hometown life --- the hollow respectability, the conspiracy of small-mindedness --- these are things I wrote about only obliquely, because they influenced me too little. I never saw them, or chose not to. In looking back, then, and setting down a few fragments, I meant to memorialize a particular time and place --- to dignify it, not disparage it --- so while our town had its murders and suicides, its embezzlers and its too-smart operators, its Injun Joes and its Boo Radleys, I felt that I would be exploiting the sorrows of others if I used these things to juice up a narrative. They did not directly influence my life.

So let me dip back into the drawer and pull out some of the old pieces. Like the women of yesterday, who kept pressed flowers and dance programs folded away in heavy books or dresser drawers, I've kept stacks of sights & sounds, hopes that lingered past their time, intentions that refuse to die. Now I lift them out and unwrap them.

Penrod Schofield, make way.

Or rather, let's go all the way back to the beginning.

FIRST LIGHT

We did not know how things came to be.
We just let the light pour in.

We had a memory
  of packing, moving from place to place, of
    olive drab and officers' tan
settling first into a cold mountain climate, then traveling
  hundreds of miles to a sun-struck tract
    just cleared from the swamp, where wild pigs
        chased out of a home
 came back nightly to search the garbage
and fat water snakes wriggled out to wait for the rats
and possums scampered across the walkways
        after dark.

In the mountains, we had lived
near the railroad track:
There, I leaned out the window
to name the cars as they passed: coal car,
tank car, box car, flat car, cattle car
    caboose
and waved at the engineer, who waved back --- I thought.

One day they could not find me.
Panic and alarums.
Half an hour later, I was discovered
below the grade
along the track
in the bushes
my face "all scratched up"
looking for an encounter, I'd guess
with my sleek steel god.
The train fascinated me beyond all else.

In that foggy mountain world, we lived with a family
that had two children, a girl, and her brother lout
who liked to beat on her.
I remember pounding his thighs
with my small fists.

He just smiled.
He had been doing it to rile me up
and watch me go crazy.

A tire swing hung in the back yard, and
the odor of burning rubber
always filled the air.

Then the Army moved us
to Louisiana, the hot zone, where there was
no more fog
no more trains
just yellow days, in
a little house on a new block;
road-grading equipment, extending our settlement daily
homeless water snakes
and wild pigs who came back to guzzle
& tump over the cans nightly.

There I met my first friend
his father also in the Army.
We played with our dump trucks, imitating
the construction we saw going on about us.

DOGTOWN, LOUISIANA

Dogs trotted down the street
  looking from side to side
  in alert friendly anticipation
  of the day's events.

They lay
  in the sun, or on the shadowed side
    of the store, or the house, or the garage ---
        panting.

In the crawl space under the porch,
  mama nursed her four or five pups
  & barked an angry warning
    to the children outside
      who tried to see.

In the town of men, the town of dogs
  ran at its heels (and wheels)
  each with its own urgencies,
    its own missions; and excitements.

At night, in the streets
 the dog world came into its own
  when a quivering intelligence,
    a higher vision, and a communicative fervor
      rose to possess them.

The moon of the streetlamp
  called to the wolf within.
    Stirred, it awoke
  and did not know where it was
and called out   for recognition.

I lay at the window, as fascinated by the dogs
    as I had been by the train

LITTLE BOYS

You push the kid down, tumble him backwards;
pride floods your head, because
          he was weak.
He deserved it because he was weak.
You only dealt him justice.

In the sun-painted streets of the new settlement,
small Army brats created a new world of their own.

"Mine!" A tug.
"No, it's mine!" A fierce tug back.
A kick.

The endless dispute over toys (Mine/No it's mine)
looked stupid to me from the beginning
and the contestants with their dim eyes
looked the same.

Where were the rewards in this world?
I'd tested it out, played its games
now my head reared back in disdain.
"Stupid" was the word that rang inside, and I wanted none of it.

So, except for my one friend, I became solitary. I had the sun and the
sky above me --- the whole wide world --- why cram myself into this
small one?

So I became the friend of dogs.

But the Korean War came to an end and my father was released
to return with us to Arkansas
to reap the benefits of peacetime.

At dusk, with the Star of Evening
and a slice of moon in the West
a neighbor might drop by and join us on the front porch:
a deep pillared space, with hanging swing
which every house had then.

The cool air laved all like a restorative bath.

As the swing creaked, the men gestured,
circling the dark air with squiggles of fire
from their lighted cigarettes.

We kids had just finished eating
as we emerged from the house.

KID WORLD

Baloney sandwich
on white bread
with lots of mayonnaise:
nothing better.

Crisp long slices
of red, spotted with
black: watermelon
on a curving green rind.

Warm mashed potatoes
overrun with gravy
& sprinkled pepper.

That's what
kids love.

July evenings:
fireflies drift & veer
& settle on the shrubbery, pulsing
while older people on the porch fan themselves
their voices
a texture of contentment and regret
as they talk about relatives, the past
and how things interwove:
how Uncle John went up north
how Mom worked at Woolworth's
and what the Depression did to Lizbeth's family.
Wasn't it hard on the Johnsons, losing their boy.
Mmm-mmm.
The fans stir.
Wars, hard times
dislocations of fate, and
the new car.
Their present state of relative ease
--- safe jobs, no war, good dinner ---
evokes a thankfulness that stops
one wary step
short of complacency.

THE SIMPLE JOYS

1. Hamburger
    Ground beef, well done,
    juice leaking
    over the onions and mustard.

2. Soft Ice Cream
    extruded, at the clerk's pull
    to fill the papery cone
    twisted
    into a coiled cylinder.
    Then --- turned upside down
    and dipped in chocolate
    which hardens into a shell!
    I paid my fifteen cents, and walked away
    kicking pebbles.

3. Warner Brothers cartoons
    The swiftness with which the gags followed
    one after another
    on Grandpa's new TV
    made them a roller coaster ride
    for a kid's nervous system.
        Bugs and Fudd
        or those surreal creatures pecking over the Moon, or Mars
        in those Dali-inspired scripts.
    These were cartoons that didn't embarrass you
        (like Casper the Friendly Ghost).
    They pointed the way to an esthetic
        of madness and inversion:
        a useful corrective
        to weighty authority.

4. Mad Magazine, before it got formulaic.
    In its rough wood-pulp pages, Kurtzman and Elder and Davis
    ripped it up and stomped on it
    delighting boys everywhere.
    No reverence, no mercy.

5. The diving board
   Run, sproing --- hurled into flight
   feeling the parts of your body
   --- hips and shoulders and head --- imbued
   with separate momentums, and struggling to coordinate them
   for a proper entry.
   The green blue splash:
   climbing out, doing it again and again The afternoons wore
                                        on;
   the hours bled
   into a trance of delight
   the water draining off my hair and shoulders as I climbed out
   for the forty-fifth time.

INNOCENT

When the breeze rises
and night laps at your feet
like a warm ocean
who could doubt
that this is the best of all possible worlds?

When night whispers to you
like an ancient motherwitch
who could think
that this world is not meant for delight?

When life calls
who could fail to follow its piping?

When the town is open for you to ramble
who could be so ungrateful
as not to embrace
not to fling his arms wide and coast down the hill, no brakes
to a transfiguration through wind and speed?

When girls
turn to you with open faces
who could hang back?
Well, you may linger a bit.
You have to figure out just what to do.

Even when great bodies of unobserved fact
bob to the surface
the wholly innocent is not daunted.
He merely ropes them in, strange fish
and puts them in tow
for later examination.

BASEBALL WEATHER

Steve looked off into the distance
and quoted a line
about "baseball weather" ---
    "Ah . . . feels like I'm floatin'."

Then I knew we were simpatico
as if any further proof were needed.

Baseball weather was when
you got the world back.
You'd been crammed into small rooms
confined between four walls
all winter.

But now, you expanded
and lapped like a warm lake
on the boundaries of everything you saw.

The Infinite Mother
loved you again
and your own love was unbounded.

Soon, the constrictions of school would fall away:
you'd look down, and see your legs in shorts
and shoes that needed no socks.

You'd build your muscles
by pumping the bicycle over hills
and carrying the golf bags for the well-to-do.

You'd spend your money at the swimming-pool.
Absorbed by the goodness of life,
you wanted the town, and the world, and your life
never to change.

That's why I never understood my contemporaries
who lusted for the prerogatives and accoutrements of adulthood
and wanted to be six years older.
"Are you crazy?" I asked,
"This is all you could ask for. This is as good as it gets."
They just shook their heads, as if
there were a message I hadn't got.

JUKEBOX REVELATIONS

Ricky Nelson, his sleepwalker's voice
bored, vacant
idling through 'Traveling Man'
and 'Young World' and 'Teenage Idol'
said one thing to us:
You see me in the magazines; you know that
I float on television and family, but
at the bottom of my well is passion, and
I want to awaken.

Roy Orbison flung his voice
to the highest registers
the limits of sorrow
seeking forgetfulness.
He was a gas flare
burning in the night, streaming over black marshes
& the wrecked barges.

The rockabilly boys
busted out of the dusty back roads
the neon Main Streets, the woodfront juke joints
of the New South. Bringers of spring and renewal,
hoodlums and church boys and hard livers,
Elvis drove Sam Phillips' convertible down Union Avenue
while Carl Perkins threw wisecracks and
young Jerry Lee pounded on the bright red side panel.

The black girls seemed to come in threes and fours, with
glossy hair, matching outfits and well-choreographed dance moves.
The Shirelles, the Marvelettes, the Chiffons:
we relished their unique pronunciations of certain words and
lived in the breath space between their larynx, lips, and palate.

We knew the very texture of their tongues
and the shape of their sinus cavities.
White boys in the suburbs, we mooned from afar
and had no idea how we would ever cross over.
But --- that rude energy! All we could do was buy their records.

The two-and-a-half minute song
was being crafted, in those years
like an engine on a workbench
running smoother, faster, wilder with each alteration.
It sung of energy, humming and directed.
It shaped our expectations of life.
Soon it would be dropped into a hot rod, connected to the drive train
and we would all roar away, bound for the highway, the skies
  California --- whatever.

LEAVING

1

The furniture had been collected in another era
and stood as a testimony of sorts.

Life had moved on, leaving artifacts.

Bedposts, turned on a lathe, had been carved to produce a series of
curves, edges, scalloped indents.
A dark heavy table, legs also lathed, ended in clawed feet, each grasping
a glass sphere. The armoire smelled of mothballs, and the dressing-table
had its many drawers.

In the corner, the rocking-chair.

The rugs were worn but still swirled and colorful. On the wall, the
clockface, with its mechanism wound daily by hand.

In the living-room, the massive piano; some cut glass. Framed photos,
tinted as they were in the 1920's.

This was working-class respectability, won by Germanic persistence in
a neighborhood where all households were well-organized, dedicated
to some hidden ideal, and the great Catholic church hulked three blocks
down the street.

In June
the winds set the lace curtains to rippling
carrying the fragrant out-of-doors into the tall rooms.
These high ceilings
this profligate use of space
valuable, per-cubic-foot space
added nothing but a feeling of elevation
to the lives below.

At the kitchen table,
Grandma tried to teach me German.
"Ein, zwei, drei, fir, funf --- "

while Grandpa worked on his handcrafts, in the garage
drilling and cutting while he talked fishing with a neighbor
and consulted his homemade oracle, the Coke-bottle barometer in a
                                             Mason jar.

I stayed there sometimes.
There was food on the table: the newspaper, and magazines --- Field
& Stream (with Ed Zern) and the National Geographic (with Jacques
Costeau). Smooth leaping bass and the blue-water tropics. What was his
boat called? The Calypso.

Night   extended this negligent idyll   into promise and mystery.

                        2

Night was an invitation;   a dark fertile vastness;   a seduction;   an all-
knowing goddess waiting with warmth, moisture, secrets;   outdoors, the
air moved, and the foliage crowded at my elbow.
Night invited me
into the wind in the trees
while I stood on the cool earth below. My chest opened   and said Yes.

Beneath the street lamps
we met
by chance
Judy, Steve, and myself
        new creatures
looking out from the cracked egg, blinking.

Now the wind-stirred vastness
held a tiny second world
in which small dramas might be played out.

3

In the empty school   in the piano room
two girls came in   as I was playing
and suddenly
  like a startled flock of birds
    like flesh rising for a kiss
      life's fertile confusion was there.

We giggled, and twisted aside
from the possibilities;
made jokes, and acted foolishly
it was all too big for us.

Three years later, in my car, another girl and her friend
made suggestions about where to go; once there, we
did little but clown; the friend offered to leave the car;
   no, no, we protested, but she did; so we went
to search for her in the woods.

            It was all still too big --- for me, at least.
            I could not find the right thing to do.

4

When, several years later   I'd found a way of understanding myself
and the world:
when I'd found a frame of reference big enough for the night
and its summons
when reading the words of experienced and truthful men
bitter unrepentant men
or coolly analytical men of elegant mien
had expanded me like a tire on its wheel-mount at the garage ---
pop! Ka-wham! --- and that small-town stuff had fallen aside ---
or so I thought ---
I returned, to wander lovingly & lost
among the streets of my former life
--- lost, not knowing if I were Here or There;
went to a basketball game, met the little sister of the Football Guy, in
the crowd, after the game --- I had never known he had one ---
made a date, and after the movie

in the car, in the hills above town
spent hours locked together --- clang! --- like two magnets
with all the mad sincerity
the naïve hunger the inexperienced openness of, I guess, youth;
did not go All The Way   not on a First Date.
These were the ways & mores of Honorable Youth
then
and actually, should be so always & forever.

But things were breaking away beneath me --- things
you never knew about --- and when you saw me at the
park   at the basketball court after I had not called for
weeks   and were happy, and called me over   I went,
holding myself standoffish   and could only say to you
that I would be leaving town in a few days

You had to turn abruptly away

BOYZ IN THE HOOD

A televised chimpanzee
  belonging to Jungle Jim or Tarzan or Sheena
  must have impressed him quite strongly
          when he was very young.

Ook, ook --- he was always smacking his lips
  hooting, and aping   the ape's slope-shouldered walk
  till you had to smile with appreciation.

There was always a deep sense of community
    between Steve and Cheetah.

He called his older brother Danny
  his 'monkey brother' and --- it was true ---
  you saw the resemblance
      once it was pointed out.

In the dusty garage
  the three brothers lifted weights, fiercely
  through cold winter, and in stifling summer
    with magazine pictures of Freddy Ortiz and Harold Poole
    tacked to the rough roof support.

It always surprised me
  how they shouted at each other   angrily, carelessly
    each remembering many past slights
      and defending against the least hint
        of territorial trespass.

The level of aggression   was high.
The old man was fierce, too.

John's father, though
  was known by all
    to be a mean son-of-a-bitch:
      an army sergeant   at a nearby post
  he made his children stand at attention
  and answer to commands
  before they sat down at the table;

he enforced military discipline
from the manual.
His children literally trembled
when he fixed his searching malevolent gaze
on them.

John's mother was timid
and driven in on herself
and seemingly disconnected   from the world.

His brother and sister
were not all that bright.

How, then, did John bloom so spectacularly?
Did his mother give him her best
before she collapsed like a spent star?
Did our circle of friends carry him through?
He was more stable than I, and had better judgment
and when I saw him last
he was the very image of the urbane liberal,
with shiny head and trimmed beard
fronting for left-moderate advocacy groups
in the statehouse
and praying for the Spirit to come down to him after dark.

Tom's father was dead
 and his mother worked in the billing office
    of a utility.
Ready for fun, good-natured, but austere as a Roman bust
 part BooBoo Bear, part Julius Caesar
   he was frighteningly willing
     to be mean
       when it suited him.
He read Aldous Huxley and was convinced
  that lawyers should run the world.
He and I had the wit
  to play off the conventions of history and literature
   and spin gloriously disrespectful jeu d'esprits
       --- Monty Pythons before our time.
      I remember his forearm
     holding the football

70

as his eyes searched for a target
  while the bodies plunged around him
    in jumbled disarray.
He and I were the underachievers   in later life.
He left law school after a month.
When you feel strongly, but know
that the world is a circus
then you must choose a path
that will not engage your passion, and thereby
suck you in.

. . . AND THE GIRL

She was Italian
living with her widowed mother
in a high-ceilinged house
from which the outdoor paint   had flaked away
& left the bare wood   to weather.

Things had begun to pile up
in the living-room
and were not removed.

She had about her
the unawakened musk
of the young Annette Funicello
from the Mickey Mouse Club.

I saw her every day
as her class passed outside the windowed door
of my history class
and she saw me.

She had
a natural goodness.
I go down on my knee
before natural goodness:
drop, and present my sword
on a pillow.

We went to some dances, and walked home
carrying books.

But our association never went further.
I was strangely frozen, and the Church's teachings
about mortal sin   did not help.

Years later
coming home
I saw notice in the paper
about her marriage, and subsequent divorce:
some oaf from the factory, I thought.
 I'd hoped for better.
I could see the clutter   & lack of opportunity
rising around her.

Then, many years later
someone sent me
a homemade periodical
stapled down the center
 in which members of the class
told their stories.
This one had hers.

She'd been rescued, or discovered, or found
by a medical doctor
from the larger world
who had taken her away
put her in a good house
and had children;
and now, well-to-do
they sailed the world
in his boat
anchoring at ports
in the Islands, and in South America.
She was happy.

Her words had the healthy sun-browned confidence
of a good life.

She'd escaped. She'd found reward

commensurate with her virtue.
He'd seen   what I saw.

I bless her with gratitude, and hope she won't mind
if I use her story here.

3

Spring-loaded for achievement,
    those of us intended for higher things   left town.
Others, not so intended, stayed.

4

    I can see
    the green uneven lot
where we played football
        weekends
    by the graveyard:
flung to earth, I came up with grass on my lips
and a roaring desire
to do it again and again.
Finally --- exhausted, desire abated --- we sprawled about.
    The sun fell lower
    and the shafts glowed brighter
as the fading autumnal light
fell more directly upon their flat stone faces
and illuminated the wings and gowns
of the motionless angels.

I can see the dusty outdoor court
  where we played, after school,
    when we'd run to get John's ball;
        played till the shadows deepened and swallowed us up.

Goodbye.
All this has the flavor
of archaic Americana now
in a world of mall rats

and music videos
and the desperate knowledge that your friends
can and will betray you
if you do not position yourself knowledgeably enough
among the vectors of cool
pulling your underwear up the required three inches
from your pants.
A carefully sculptured attitude
of brutish banality
 is called for.
I guess we came in
at the tail end of the good years.
James Dean was still
a talisman to conjure with.
Ray Charles, Sam Cooke,
and the new boys --- John Lennon and the
Lads from Liverpool.

5

The Church   ---   benevolent
   deceptive
      richly beautiful
         loomed above us all like
            the Cosa Nostra.

All the arts
   of doctrinal terrification
    and physical whacking
      designed to keep
        the Dublin mob of street urchins
          under control
       designed to keep
       Seamus from impregnating Mary
         till he could hold a job at the mill
           were brought over, and practiced
             on a population already well-behaved.
Seamus needed to be hit over the head with a shovel,   and often.
He was thick as a brick.

In spring, the children marched outside the church   and up the
aisle   bearing branches and flowers   singing to the Queen of the
May. Bunches and sprays with bindings of vine torn from field and
garden were placed before her statue. The windows were thrown open,
and the breezes blew through. The priest advanced with slow stately
steps, swinging the censer; the boys bore the grand candles. Oh Mary
we crown thee with blossoms today . . .

The thick dark fabrics
the wrought gold instruments of celebration:
all these were fascinating, and suggested hidden mysteries
but the real center of theological gravity   for me   lay in the tales
not of martyrs' blood
or of dubious miracles wrought by hundred-year-old bodyparts
but of the monk glimpsed in his solitary cell, hovering in mid-air
in the grips of the divine ecstasy.

I knew I would experience that   one day.

As one goof among many, Tom and I wrote a bogus hagiography
   --- the Life of St. Ubaldus ---
a hollywoodish treatment, filled with purring pious cynicism
Youth, Suffering, Fall, and Redemption:
Wizard-of-Oz-ish miracles, and
the dying sinner/saint picked up and enfolded in the arms
of the saintly abbot Odo of Cluny.

No wonder the world set its grim face against us.
We were such smart-asses.

6

        Steve could not leave behind
the downfield run, the tackle, and the threshing frenzy   to break free
so he took up rugby, and toured England
with a Yank team, thrashed by the Brits
at every stop, and treated to drinks afterwards.
How I would have loved to have seen that.
He called me   a couple of years ago
and said, 'You used to write --- why don't you send me something?'

I'd fallen   into a gray kick-the-can despondency:
I had all these pieces lying around
  some half-finished, others filed away;
and, yeah,
   I'd half given up;
but, I couldn't disappoint Steve;
so I began to knock some words together
with a serious intent.
So, as it turns out, the unmentioned good I'd done
back then, in my home town   had trickled through the circuits of the
world
and come back to save me   just as despairing Saint Ubaldus
had been saved by the packets of holy seeds he'd handed out
in his youth.
Unbeknownst to him, they had
"sprouted goodness
throughout Europe"
and sent Odo of Cluny
donkey-riding,
searching for their source.

7

So some good comes back.
Other times, though, the Devil
will weave a web of impenetrable silk
around the good you've done
vainly it flutters its wings
because nothing pleases the Devil so
as to see good batter itself senseless
slide down, exhausted, and surrender.
He caps the candle.
As the curl of smoke   rises from the wick
he does a spirited, flashy dance
and all his allies in the world
feel the news, and are heartened.

WORKSHOP

Coffee cans (Folger's, Maxwell House)
rattling with nails
mason jars full of nuts, bolts, and screws,
the smell of dust and grease;
oil-pot and grease-can and dry-rags.
I twist the cold handle of the vise
to watch its screw-mounted jaws open and shut.
On the backboard from rows of projecting nails
hang pipe wrench, crescent wrench, and box wrenches;
cutters and grabbers and twisters
hand-operated drills with reeling gears,
rows of boring bits
a toothed sawblade tightened in a rectangular frame.

Grandfather in overalls
corded arms, mobile like an ape's, supple
hanging like an ape's when not in use; his mouth open
guileless face open
all of him   an open door into the hallways of the past;
the particle-swarm from then
still blowing out of the open door of now.

      The past was alive in him, in that garage:
    would it ever
  speak to me?
        Never quite did.

My choice to become a skilled laborer, or craftsman
though necessary, can be construed
as a kind of loyalty to a kind of life
which I understood, and which was not abhorrent to me;
for in leaving college, I had tumbled back into the substratum
from which two generations of focused toil
had sought to deliver me.

Now I go out to the garage

to cut & sand & rout
or just hide out, while I listen
to the good jazz.
I've added, you see
to the basic format.

On the wall, a Turner print
 and Elvis.

But a brown-tinted picture of my old grandpa
would not be out of place
in a corner, above a workbench altar
and a museum of oiled antique tools.

WOOD PANELING, WITH DUCKS

Framed ducks, on the wall:
settling into the water
or rising from it.

The cheery glow of the shaded lamp
falls over the shellacked wood grain
and the tinted pine radiates
the orange-brown warmth of a richer wood.

It is the kind of room in which men
have a few drinks
before setting out.

There's a big dog
moaning eagerness
on the porch.

Cold and dark: the gray dawn
is a good hour away.

Into the truck, and on to the river.
Out among the tall grasses.

I could tell another story now, but it would be Nick Adams', not mine.

There was something about it all I couldn't grasp. An essential eluded
me. The men were in on it. I was willing, but something never
clicked. I was an alien: not really interested. A good shot, but
I preferred inanimate targets. My father did his best, but I was already
made another way.

I dreamed about the Cambrian, the Ordovician, the Silurian, the
                                                        Devonian
            ancient Paleozoic seas
            and the near-brainless creatures, armored and clawed
            that swam through them
        or the crinoids that waved slowly in the currents.

All of this was hard to explain
to purposeful and practical men
with faces remote
and filled with blunt simplicity.

Z

Zorro was my role model:
after watching a few televised episodes
I left the Z mark
on two dozen frosted windowpanes
in the grade-school classroom.

Master swordsman, man of culture and refinement
he posed as a fop
to better reconnoiter
the lay of the land
and discover how he could best thwart, and overturn
the Evil Commandante.

Tolerated by men by day, and snubbed by luscious Latin sweeties
by night he emerged on his fierce black horse
to right wrongs, and leave his mocking mark
on those who served tyranny, and were slower
with their wits or sword-arm.

This seemed better by far to me than other boys' dreams
of becoming baseball pitchers
or John Wayne, killing Indians.

I felt keenly
his father's disappointment in him:
time and again, Don Alejandro
muffled his expressions of disgust
out of family respect.

When the aging Don bent over the wounded Zorro
but refrained from removing his mask
my heart leaped up in my throat:
wouldn't his father <u>ever</u> understand
who he really was?

ELVIS 1

He was a good boy
    drove a truck
to support his Mama and Daddy
    honest, respectful
he played gospel
    at the piano
      on Sunday evenings.

    But the jumping rhythm
    of the black-skinned bop
had got into his leg
and turned that nerve
    from toe to head
      to a live wire.

ELVIS 2

To the mill owners
 the grandees
  the architects
   of the New South
  he was raw material
  his hungry belly
 would send his body
 to barter its strength
to power the gears
of metal fab and petrochem
construction and transport.

To the Junior Chamber of Commerce
 and their rattle-brained wives
 building a new world
of suburbs car lots and daughter debutantes
 he was genetic inferiority personified
  come out of the past
  to haunt them. They
   looked at him
    with population control
     on their minds.
They would scrape out the pot of Dixie:
  use, then discard the rime ---
   his kind.

But he evaded the dull blow
 that was coming his way.
 Stepped aside, and into
  a shaft of clear light
  a clear space
  where he could move
   without obstruction.

ROCKABILLY

Big loose-limbed boys who don't know no limits
    got their hair slicked back
     their cool manly ways
   they heard Elvis and said,
      "That's me."

Good boys, respectful boys who loved their Mama
        worked hard
     knew right from wrong
   they heard Elvis and dropped what they were doing
       said, Mama I'm sorry
     but history's a-calling me.
          Where's my guitar?
         Hey, let's bop!

Bad boys, good boys   all tore loose
  left the farm
    the store
     the truck-drivin' job
    jumped the fence
  and ran for daylight.

NEWSPAPER

Held in its tight roll by a rubber band
flung, and bounced to a stop on the grass,
 the newspaper
     is a daily treat.

We scoop it up
     run up the steps,
          and spread it on the living-room rug.

Open to the funnies, first.
  Our paper doesn't have
     the good ones, no Pogo, or Li'l Abner,
        or Smokey Stover.
           We'll have to make do with
               Steve Canyon and Dick Tracy
                  and his gallery of malformed criminals.

                    But
               the big single-panel
           'Our Boarding House' with Major Hoople
        and Martha, and the boarders, and the nephews
     --- "Uncle Bulgy, I mean Amos" ---
     that's the one   we really like.

               Elsewhere, the paper warns us
           about communism, and liberals, and labor unions
               misguided soft-headed policies
                  university intellectuals
                    and we nod, sagely.
                       We'll be good.
                       We'll be loyal.
                       We'll never go for
                          any of that stuff.

THE WAR

The memory, or the fact, or the smoke, or the drama of WWII
  still hung in the air
    still lived in the minds
      of the men who drove to work every day
and the women who tended their new & growing households.

      Memories of Italy and the Pacific Islands
        barracks and bivouac
          trucks and backpacks
            served as referents, and,
      when the men played poker
even a child could see that they were back in the Army again.

      To them, Hemingway was a god
    with square-cut face and trimmed beard
          an Odin, who had been to war,
            who loved hunting and fishing, as they did,
            and now presided over Asgard, from the Gulf
    while General Ike, of Normandy,
      ruled the nation from Washington on his behalf.

      In summer, they went to a two-week camp
       to march and drill and drive jeeps
    & re-learn how
    to elevate the big guns to hit the far hill.

      In the meantime, a new downtown of glass and plastic
      had been added to the old one of brick. We kids
      ran crazily through this new world.

      When we went to the magazine racks, we saw
    bright cover paintings
          of scarred virile Yanks
          carrying off screaming Nazi babes
          legs kicking
          as the shells burst in the sky.
          Men's War. True Guts.
      True, these magazines were for half-wits;
      our fathers didn't read them;

that made them easier for us to snicker at.

Then, one day, a bland-faced man came to the house:
his hair was combed in wavelets.
He and my father had a long talk, and he gave my father
a stack of pamphlets.
The two nodded thoughtfully, and my father
came to me and
pointed out that Mad Magazine, of which I then had a copy,
was being written in New York City by enemies of the nation
to inculcate disrespect for America, for its institutions, and for the Army
in particular.
I was shown particular panels and features that proved this.

I could see the smallness and the lack of comprehension in their eyes.
For the first time in my life I was embarrassed for another.
Someone had just pulled a brick out of a wall, and a clear impartial light,
which I did not particularly like, now shone through.

Where was their sense of humor?

More family history? Then I'm arrogating an importance to myself I don't deserve. The reader will say: who does this guy think he is? I've become like the bore who makes himself real by inflicting his dullness on you while you look around for avenues of escape. So let's get this straight. I am nobody, absolutely nobody, and of no importance. I am neither a TV star nor a pro athlete nor a talk-radio ragemeister. I have not overcome bulimia or survived a childhood of abuse. What I am is a careful detective on the trail of the American character, and I mean to call softly to it & coax it out of its hiding-place --- or call it down from its self-promoting battlements --- to examine what's become of it, see what's been lost and what remains, what's entered and what has departed, and in this quest I have to use what I know.

One is fortunate in having had two sets of grandparents --- close by, easily visited. Settled into rocking-chairs, drifting slowly into decrepitude, they were like living histories, tarnished weather-vanes still pointing in a forgotten direction.

2: Pioneers

My mother came from the Irish, and she grew up on the far side of town, where residences were sparse and woodlands began to predominate. Actually she was half-Irish, but she denied her father's influence and so became her mother's child. The story behind that rift, part social and part familial, is part of our country's forgotten history and sprawls in all its wretched idiocy across several generations.

Let me take a few pages from a family history. The prose may not meet our current standards of elegance, but --- lumpy as stew --- the beef and bone are there.

*   *   *

My grandfather on my mother's side was a farmer from a long line of poor farmers whose origins were lost & forgotten somewhere on the shifting frontier, somewhere on that advancing front of felled trees, patchwork cultivation and backwoods settlements that pushed out from Virginia through the Cumberland Gap after the Revolution and salted the Kentucky hills with the descendants of indentured servants. The forward-looking, the well-to-do, and the well-connected had already taken the bluegrass country, and were on their way to becoming a regional aristocracy; the hills were left to the poor, with their dogs, their deer rifles, and their swaying wagons.

My grandfather's name was Martin Luther Sewell, and his father was George Washington Sewell, and one might say that the names tell it all. Although their surname is Welsh, with its hint of Celtic sinuosity, their given names have all the bony rectitude of the Protestant farmer holding fast to first principles and refusing all alien temptations.

This does seem to have been the key to George W. Sewell's character, for he was rigidly abstinent in a country known for its mountain stills and clandestine pressed-corn economy. He did not drink, or gamble, or tell the sly barnyard joke; he refused to sink into the muck of tobacco-juice-spitting commonness. Celebration and vulgarity were alike strangers to him; let the others sing, dance, or play the fiddle, or bet on horses, dogs, or elections. To hold himself fast to duty, and to avoid falling into dissipation as so many others had, he built his life around the hard-bench church, with its Bible-reading Methodism, around the weekly meetings of a little denomination unleavened by the excesses of the travelling revivalist: sobriety was their claim to respectability, so they felt no need to holy-roll or shout. My mother, who was raised

97

in the same house as her elderly grandparents, did not like them; the barrenness and sternness of their unloving personas put her off. The old lady chopped at her ankles with a cane; the old man forbade her to touch his books.

I do not believe, upon careful consideration, that my great-grandfather was unloving; only that he had a short supply; he could not include more than his one son and one grandchild in the circle of his love, and that grandchild was not my mother. She was left out.

I knew George Washington from his picture which hung on my grandparents' bedroom wall --- bony, stern, ferocious, with well-trimmed white Civil War whiskers; his wife, seated next to him, seemed trapped in the 19th century with nowhere to go. I knew him from my mother's reminisces, and from his many possessions, which still littered my grandparents' house, and blended with my grandfather's, for the two had shared a common life on a Texas farmstead till my grandfather was twenty-eight, and then on an Arkansas farm till he was thirty-five.

LIFE OF GEORGE WASHINGTON SEWELL
AND HIS SON, MARTIN LUTHER

1

Orphaned as a child, in the 1840's, and raised by his older sister in the hills of Kentucky, George Washington Sewell had almost no property; his two older brothers sold what little inheritance they had and headed west, leaving a cabin and a bit of money for their younger sister and brother. They were never heard from again. From childhood, G. W. had had to hire out on other men's farms, working for wages and bargaining for his sustenance through the winters; his sister married quickly, as soon as the opportunity arose. The choice of becoming a ne'er-do-well, a lowlife, a propertyless drifter, a drunkard, or . . . something better . . . must have pressed upon him keenly. To keep himself from sliding along the path of least resistance, and to preserve some sort of hope for a future life, G. W. relied on the church as others would their family. While other young fellows, whose fathers owned farms, might play lewd games with the girls in the hayloft, and then be forced to marry at nineteen, G. W. could afford no such license; he had no property or family to fall back on. He must have acquired a reputation as a dependable worker, because in his middle 30's he married a widow who had come into a farm she could not tend.

Ada Addison, the wife of his late adulthood, was almost five years older than himself; still they managed to have two children. Their first child they named Ida; at the age of one year, she died after eating her first blackberries. The horror of it --- losing his daughter, after waiting a lifetime for her, and then rejoicing in her for a year --- seems to have inflicted a lifelong trauma on G. W.

Their second child was Martin Luther. Perhaps by so naming him, GW was asking God to spare him; maybe the name would firm him up, make him a tough little bugger who'd not be swept away so easily.

When Martin was two --- in 1882 --- the Sewells sold their Kentucky farm and bought virgin land in Texas. In all likelihood the railroads had advertised, seeking to capitalize on their generous land grants; and when the Sewells read the descriptions of flat, untouched prairie land from which a crop had never been taken it seemed a gift from God --- fertile land, easily cultivated, too good to pass up. They arranged a purchase, sold all but their essentials, and traveled, either by wagon or by rail, to an undeveloped patch of north Texas.

But somehow the expected bounty failed to materialize. The enormous, open, flat land was largely indifferent to their efforts. The sun set each evening, orange in the west, after the Sewells had busted sod all day behind a hand-held plow; this was in an era when the more successful farmers were buying twenty-blade harrows pulled by teams of horses. There was something about the land, or its position on the rainfall map, that made it unresponsive, unfriendly, that made it resistant. The crops they had raised so easily and knowledgeably in the Kentucky hills would not grow here, or grew only sparsely; and the Sewells did not have the money to build up a grazing herd, or to follow the mechanized lead of their more successful neighbors. The clouds drifted over without dropping their bounty; certainly the dust storms blew in twice a year, and blew on through, leaving the red-yellow dust and taking the black. Gradually the Texas farm changed from GW's promised land to his Calvary. He and his family "all but starved", to quote my mother.

In Washington, the presidents rolled on by --- Cleveland, Hayes, McKinley --- while in Texas the farmers gathered to hold meetings to denounce those who held papers on their land, and to demand relief from deflationary policies, and to excoriate the politicians who voted with the banker rather than the farmer. There is no suggestion that George Washington participated in any of the agitation of his time; there is ample proof he continued to hold fast to first principles, that is, to spend his Sundays in the little church where hellfire, temperance, heavenly reward, and anti-Catholicism were preached. His wife and son, without a doubt, occupied the same pew.

During the 1800's, anti-Catholicism had become a mainstay of American Protestant preaching; the Pope was said to be stretching his wine-bloody hands across the Atlantic, seeking to seize the United States --- much was made, by way of analogy, of a Restoration king's intrigues with the Vatican --- and the immigrant Catholics, landing in the East, were said to constitute the Pope's army. Did he not already have all of Latin America? Circuit-riding preachers had alarming tales to tell. Priests were said to kidnap Protestant girls, and hold them in nunneries where they raped them repeatedly; nuns, accomplices, kept the girls behind locked doors. Bogus texts, allegedly dictated by escapees, were sold after the services. Awe-struck farmers thumbed through them; their jaws dropped. The circuit-riding preachers were part showman, part vigilante, but all American --- they were the talk radio jocks of their day --- and George Washington, duly alarmed, wanting above all else to be a moral man and a good citizen, became an anti-Catholic bigot.

2

During these years Martin Luther Sewell did not enjoy much of what we would call a social life; in this old age, when I knew him, he still had the lonely light about him, of a man who had spent his formative years looking far, far away at the horizons of an unpeopled land. We may assume he rose before dawn; that he walked the rows, jerked along by the mule; that he harvested by hand, with sack and wagon. As he came into physical adulthood he could not help but see his parents' slow decline. I once had a photograph of him from his early 20's: prematurely bald, he nevertheless had the flashing eye and confident stance of a man who knows he will grasp his dreams and inhabit them, whatever those dreams might be: a man who knows he will prevail. Whatever became of that young man I do not know; probably he was contained bit by bit and then worn away, for every decision he made had to take first the farm and then his parents into consideration. He had his parents to care for, and without the farm he was nothing. But every year the farm was more of a losing proposition.

After several disappointing years the three of them must have conceded that this farm was not going to support them, much less a second family, as the older two became less able. They decided to sell while they still could, and move to Arkansas, to the hills, to a land like the one G. W. had come from.

I suppose it is a tribute to their persistence that the land was never taken away from them; that they were able to sell and carry away enough money to try again.

But once again, the prospects were better than the reality; by the time they got there, the good land had been snapped up. Again they struggled, this time for eight years, before giving it up. The soil was too thin, the rocks too plentiful. Jokes were told, stories were circulated in the southwest at about this time, about how rocky the land in the Arkansas hills was; but GW had never had his ear to the jokesters' grapevine.

Martin Luther assumed family responsibilities. He heard a mailman's job was open in a nearby town, to be awarded by competitive examination. Teddy Roosevelt had just reformed the civil service, and

101

government jobs were being given out on a merit basis. ML took the exam and won the job. He moved to town, took a room in a boarding house, and arranged to sell the farm. With the proceeds, he bought a small house for himself and his parents. Until he died, the mail buggy and the leather pouch --- later the motorized mailcar --- would earn him and his a better living than either of the farms ever had.

3

When he moved to town, he was still unmarried, a man of thirty-five, just as his father had been. In young men, the tide of love & lust conjoined carries what is best in them to the fore, but this tide in Martin Luther must have risen and splashed away without reaching any of its intended goals; at thirty-five he had quite possibly not yet known woman. Any man in his position would carry with him many memories --- wistful, incandescent, or fevered --- of imaginary trysts with women seen briefly at church or at a train station in town, women whose appearance took his heart away and who lived with him thereafter in his memory and longing. Now, in town, he was no longer young, but he could still marry, for now he had a steady, good-paying job, and a small wood-frame house in a decent enough neighborhood.

At the boarding house he had met a farm girl, also recently come to town, who had begun to train as a nurse; she was not exactly a girl, but a woman of thirty, still unmarried. Their similarity in background drew them together. Both had come to town to start a new life, yet both looked back to the farm, the only life they had ever known. If ML was to marry and have any children, she was his one --- and probably his last --- chance.

There was only one trouble: she was an Irish Catholic.

What terrible arguments must have riven the Sewell family before Martin's marriage, we will never know, but certainly can imagine. In all likelihood the desire for progeny trumped all, for Martin was realistic enough to know that there were not that many women of childbearing years who would look favorably upon him; the lonely halo of the prairie farmer still encircled his head and marked him to all who met him as a man out of his element, as a farmer come to town, a man whose intelligence had been sealed behind the numbed, inarticulate persona which daylong solitary labor creates. His father understood Martin's need to marry, and agreed regretfully to what was to him a hateful compromise.

102

Mary Flynn, though a country girl born and raised, was in many ways the exact opposite of Martin Luther Sewell. Laughing and playful, she was the oldest girl in a prolific family; the younger ones had always been put in her care. Whereas Martin's first memories were of the desolate prairie farmstead, hers were of a large, good-natured family who thrived on love but were just too numerous to make inheritance an option. He hungered for human contact; she had it coming out of her fingertips. He was cadaverous, an American Gothic; she was sly and jolly, an Irish Catholic. They married and she went to live with him in the small house where his parents quickly revealed themselves to her as her enemies and persecutors in a war of religion she had not expected or asked for.

Her husband did not defend her. He sided with his parents. Given his name, he may have felt it his duty to hound the Church of Rome. With them, he insisted that she convert to Methodism, but she saw nothing appealing in a religion that defamed Catholics so badly, that is, that lied about her own father and brothers, and made these lies an article of faith, and huddled about these lies in mock-defense of American liberty. So loud arguments --- demands and refusals --- began to fill the air.

Before she and Martin stopped sleeping together, they had two daughters. Despite the older Sewells' insistence that the girls be raised Methodist, both elected to become Catholics. It was simply a choice between human sweetness --- for the Flynns were indeed the sweetest people that ever lived --- and Gothic scariness.

Yet it was not that simple. When the first girl was born, old George Washington announced that she was his little Ida come back; he doted on her. When my mother was born, a year later, he paid her no mind. He had his little Ida back; that was all he needed, all that mattered.

And George Washington had another hidden dimension to him, one which finally revealed itself fully in his old age; for during those years working for other men in the Kentucky hills, and for his own on the prairie farm, GW had nurtured a hidden literacy. Books --- such classics as were allowed to circulate in 'the Sahara of the Bozart' --- were his secret retreat. No Chaucer, no Boccaccio, but he had bought his own copy of the Divine Comedy, the one with the frightening Dore engravings. I used to inspect it as a child, peeping reluctantly --- albeit repeatedly --- at the terrifying Inferno.

My mother says that in his retirement he would sit on the front porch and read Dickens --- one novel after another --- "He didn't read any trash" she says. When she told me this, I then saw him in full. He could not help but return to Dickens again and again because Dickens' tales of poor boys, orphaned, struggling against the odds, were his own story. Dickens understood him.

In his possessions I also found Guy de Maupassant and Victor Hugo.

He had held himself aloof from the life around him, in the Kentucky hills, because the course of life set out for him, as a landless boy, was a sure slide into worthlessness. The church had been his lifesaver; he had thrown himself into its world of Sunday services and weeknight meetings and summer picnics because only the church spoke of the light from above, and offered him a radical equality with other men in that light. He had married a widow from the same church. Surely the church would never betray him. So when the church began to talk about the Papists and the dangers they presented, and to make that its main Sunday drawing-card, he could not help but spring to its defense; he hadn't the sophistication to pry apart the preachers' claims; he was unable to understand that the merchants of paranoia had penetrated the Rock of Ages and were playing him.

5

During the years from 1918 through 1935, Martin accomplished what were to me some amazing things. Since he, his parents, and his wife were all farm people, and still longed to find some use for their skills, he bought five acres of land outside town and began to build on it what to my child's eye, many years later, was a stone castle, while he farmed a part of the rest. When the Depression came, he continued to build, bit by bit, paying the stone-masons load by load and layer by layer. He and his wife raised chickens, kept a cow and planted an orchard. They plowed and sowed a half-acre. When the house was completed, all two-and-a-half stories, he sold the small wood-frame house and moved his family in. His mother had just died, at ninety-two; his father, GW, was eighty-eight.

My mother remembers GW as a tough old bird, who even at ninety years of age would walk three miles into town for an afternoon in the town's movie theatre, watching Tom Mix or Hoot Gibson. Before the move, he had always taken his reborn 'Ida' to walk to the store with him; now, occasionally, she would walk with him, even though she was eleven or twelve years of age and the walk was not a short one. Between his chair of the front porch, his Dickens, his granddaughter Ida, and the plowed half-acre out back, GW's world was as complete as it could be in the absence of his wife.

That was the house my mother grew up in.

As I wrote this, the past --- GW, his fierce devotion and faith misplaced,
the untilled prairie, the belief in the future, weary days and the hopes
sparsely fulfilled --- the past, with its broken wheels, its travels
and start-overs, rose up in me like a drowned body from a murky
bayou. Spirit hovered over the waters. As I reflected on our family's lost
or lingering history I wrote this reverie.

(untitled poem)

In part we are creatures of our times; in part we are
a green stalk from an old root sliding unnoticed into new surroundings.
In part we are the past, corrupted somewhat; in part, we are the moment;
and, partly, we live outside time: a dervish, or an angel with a pipeline to
God.

We know our jobs, and how to do them;
  we know the people we work with, and we
     have come to know the television
        and its schedule
         a little too well.
     We read the offers that arrive daily in the mail,
chiefly from credit card companies that want to enslave us.
        Some of the opportunities of our times we have
      embraced, and made ours,
      others we have let pass us by.

Life had obliged us
to find a niche, to cut and dig
like the nesting crab, to pull over us as many debris
as it takes to cover us:
a decorative hunk of coral
home entertainment equipment
cleverly made little pieces
resting on the shelf
a pleasingly arranged living room

and, in the garage
outdoor barbecue, propane stove
inflatable swim stuff ---
whatever it takes
to cover us.

Each day, we walk from the mailbox to the front door
flip through the daily stack of letters
unlock the door close it behind us
continue to inspect the envelopes
looking for the letter --- we don't know what
that never arrives.
As we open the blinds late afternoon sun slants in
and takes us once again to the living-room of
our childhood, our first home. At a time like this
      we might ask
What is our relation to the past?
How does it live on?
Does it guide us like a mute angel?
Or does it live on, like a blind and baffled beast
      on a chute to nowhere?

*   *   *

Well, old GW and Martin Luther live on within me. Their house, in which I spent so much of my childhood, was haunted by relics, by empty rooms, by the afternoon sun, by ghostly rectitude, by GW's imposing portrait, and all his scattered leavings which turned my mind toward the prairie farmstead I'd never seen. As I rummaged through trunks that had not been opened for sixty years, and paged through the engraved advertisements for plows and harrows and reapers, the gentle odor of mold and decay came to be to me the very essence of the past, a sweet private perfume; and, as I read his stacks of temperance literature, GW came to inhabit my mind as the very embodiment of a certain American character.

In school, years later, I was to discover William Jennings Bryan and then my feeling for the period was augmented, filled out. Bryan had an honest heart and his Cross of Gold speech was dead-on. It does not matter that Darrow made a fool of him over evolution, or that Mencken despised him. The Great Commoner represented the farmer before the nation, and the farmers, at that time, were seventy per cent of the American population. My grandfather even looked like Bryan, the same shiny bare skull, the same woven fan and pitcher of ice-water (I had seen a TV dramatization of <u>Inherit the Wind</u>), the same penchant for losing himself in Biblical prophecy. But Bryan had a gregarious nature and that my grandfather never could share.

Late in his 70's, Martin went poking through the hedges with his cane and upset a nest of wasps, which swarmed out and stung him so severely that he fell, pitching against the hedge as he went down, thus calling forth more wasps. Mary found him with the insects hovering, yellow and vicious in the summer sun, and pulled him back as best she could and called an ambulance. He mended from the heart attack and lived another decade, sustained by the knotty horse-bone constitution that years of farm labor and letter-carrying had created. When at last he did die it was neither quick nor easy.

CARD GAMES

Many a morning I sat opposite him
playing checkers on the board he'd crafted
he in his rocking-chair, I in mine.
Sometimes we'd play 'authors', a simplified variant
of go fish, its ancient cards illustrated with bordered portraits
of novelists and historians
and a list of books each had written.
(I've since read Hardy and Howells, but
I've wondered about "Coniston" and "The Crisis".)
Apparently, writers were more valued
in those entertainment-deprived days.
One cannot imagine a popular game today
featuring Mailer, Roth, Sebald, and Ballard.

My grandmother, on the other hand, used a deck of cards
from the nineteenth century --- an 'alphabet' deck,
illustrated with cornucopias and chubby angels and sheaves of flowers
to play a spelling game, drawing cards and making words and laying
them down.
As we played, she nattered on, twenty words for every one I uttered
but that was all right, because her voice, soft, cajoling, sweet, was
like the fluid rushing and bubbling of a brook --- a voice like her
brothers' who came to visit, singly, about once a year.
When I grew up, I discovered: this was how the Irish spoke.

My grandfather, though, said very little.
Instead, he seemed to be always on the verge
of saying something he could not get out. It was as if
he'd run up against the wall of articulation and pressed his face
against the glass
but could go no further.
His mouth dropped open, the need to communicate was in his eye,
but
nothing came.
These moments were frequent but brief, for then he would snap back
into his customary dignity.
He'd prevailed, but that had not been enough.
His army'd run away. Now he was sealed inside.

He'd lost the wars of religion, but
we were sitting in his stone castle, on his five acres.
Now he just wanted to know his grandchildren.

I did not know it then, but I was the occasion
for their household to knit back together
somewhat.

There had been no children in the house for twenty years.
The couple had lived in the spent shell of their exploded past,
a barren marriage.
Now, by playing cards with the new child, and checkers, and telling
little stories
of the distant past, they cast a comforting spell over my life
and must have retrieved something of their own.

My grandfather received each of his grandchildren open-handedly:
a better man than his own father, George Washington.
In exile, I suppose, he'd learned to value what he'd missed.

My grandfather released a corner of his five acres for his daughter and my father to build upon, so in a year his stone castle had a more modern offspring, spaced well away. That was where I came to live, after four years under his roof and a year of moving with the army.

As the rising tide of prosperity came in to lift all boats, the surrounding hills and woods were bought up by the developers, divided into lots and remade into the new suburbs, with concrete driveways and brick outer walls and no porches. His house and land remained an anachronism, a country gentleman's estate behind a hedged barrier, with woods and field and chicken-house.

And thus we have the setting for the 'poems' I've not yet printed.

3: Storing Up The Fat

BLACKBERRIES

1

When the wide world
simmered in the July sun
and the woods bleached and fattened
then my sister and I would leave the house and
pick a path through the tall grasses
to the blackberry bushes --- with our pails, and
push aside the stickers, to
reach in and grab the ripe clusters.

Always, a box turtle was twisting his neck up
to tear off what sweet bits he could.
Always, the brambles left little droplets of blood on my wrists.

Pails full, we returned to the house to roll the berries in sugar and eat
them immediately.

2

In this July cauldron of heated air
the clouds towered up on all sides, leaving the sky open.
Mighty as statues of gods, their puffed-stone billows
glowed cream and orange
with the sun's trapped light. Like presences, they looked down on us as
they circled and drifted.

As the daylight ebbed,
the clouds left and right would light up inwardly
with electrical discharges,
signaling each other across the summer distances.

3

We had few duties, and little or no place
in the adult world of necessity. What we did
did not matter. What remained of the farm

was an anachronism: the chicken house was emptied, but
the plowing, planting, picking and canning went on
on a shrinking patch. Potatoes, melons, tomatoes, okra, string beans, and peas
are what I remember.

What was left, then
and what swallowed us up
was the all-conquering world of
nature: budding and breeding, it
filled every inch of space with leaves
and tall trees unmolested.
Fallen branches were quickly devoured by worms, ants, and fungi
clearings filled with brambles
and wire fences were covered with vines and pierced by saplings
as life swarmed up in a celebration of itself.

Unfortunately, we did not take the other world
the world outside our little preserve
as seriously as we should have.
Our grandfather's stone castle
three stories on one side, two on the other
was a fortress that held it off.
So when we finally recognized the real world
of school and commerce
cabal and whispered gossip
significant glances and unspoken plans
for the power it was
we had a lot of catching up to do.

I had enough panache to go after it
to win or make my place,
but I was still a dumb bungler, running into walls and
saying, "Whaaat?"

MEET THE CAT

1

The shining streets are empty:
heat has slammed down on the earth
like a card-player
who holds the winning combination
and means to show it decisively. The heat wins.

In the liquid brightness far from the highway
in the half-wooded acres
I run my finger down the spine of a sensitive plant
to watch the spread leaves fold, and close.
Its flower is a pink sunburst
dusted with gold: a low, thor ny bush.

In a similar heat, on other days
I have run my finger down the spine of a hor ned lizard, over and again
to watch him flatten
and 'doze', peaceful. His spiky head falls lower and lower.
His body spreads
like a pancake.

2

High on its pillars
my grandfather's sleeping-porch overlooked his acres
like a galleon's foredeck would overlook the waves.
Its screened space contained a spindly bed, and on it
I lay, as the breezes passed over, reading a weekly newsmagazine
about Eisenhower and Khrushchev.
Years later, reading a line in a Bradbury story
   --- about the sea-captain & the wheat like an ocean below his high
porch ---
I was lifted, and carried as on a warm holy wind.

On those hot days
as I walked through the tall grasses
between the wood and the field

great yellow and black plated grasshoppers
   magnificently armored, knights of the mandible
      would launch themselves on long sailing arcs
         whirring and clicking   as they glided over
            me, and their grasstop forest.

On those hot days
   the red-capped woodpecker rattled the air
   as he beat at the high dead tree
      his persistent body visible in silhouette
between the trunk and the sky.

But I had to awaken
   from this lovely, lonely sun-drenched trance.
      Indeed, I had tarried far too long.

                    3

         L, her tough little working-class face
      pale wax-like lipstick
limbs perfect, toasted brown

         "Quarter to Three" on the jukebox
invited me to a fantastic world of adulthood and excess
a cavernous wonder

The brink of mystery:
excess and wonder.

I pedaled my bike   across town
   to a new rendezvous
      while around me, the hills rose and fell.

Now, the heat   was no longer a card-player
   but a big cat
      breathing, drowsing, powerful
         which had settled invisibly upon the town;
            the dreams in his knowing and somnolent head
               would soon become mine
                  as he awakened and stretched
                     and saw through my eyes.

L, her jaunty & heedless stride,
piston legs in white shorts
my finger running down the spine of the sensitive plant

Now
a deep purring growl   emanated insensibly   from all around:
the secret of all life
was calling
from a new and more urgent realm.

TORNADO WEATHER

The flat-bottomed thunderheads
float in on gray muzzy hulls
carrying their towering cumulonimbus riders.

A cold wind springs up.
It blows along the ground
and flings the birds, struggling, into the trees,
whose leaves are upended and ravished
as if their skirts had blown up.

Nature is preparing
another sweet outrage
another tornado season.

In the peace that falls between cold gusts,
all things grooved and detailed
stand out in uncanny precision
in the coppery light.

Then the wind resumes, and it has some water in it.
Our mother stands at the door, urging us inside,
too soon, I think, to enjoy the real fun.

When the Biblical darkness falls, and the white lights
crash and boom, we are in the basement, on our knees,
praying the rosary under her direction.

Above, the pagan godheads
float and cavort on the disturbed airways
laugh, and slap the land down to watch us scurry and hide.

Let them do their worst.

We had taken the land from <u>them</u>, and if they
returned every now and then, just to fright us,
we knew that by morning they would be
emptied   their clothing of cloud fallen
and would slip back unseen to their hideaways
--- their mountain fortresses --- whatever.

This was a Christian land now,
orderly and God-fearing
with steeples (occasionally struck by lightning)
tall grain silos, and long ribbons of highway

READING MATERIAL FOR THE LAD

It was that time in life
when you wanted to let the spirit of invention
out of its box
watch it take wings
then run along on the ground below, leaping as if to join it.

If you read, SF was just the thing.
The 'serious' novelists might be recording
the slow grinding down of a man
the extinction of his marriage
his self-betrayal at work
and so on --- what kid
at the threshold of life wants
to read this?

But antic play, savage inventiveness, and
the exuberant or frightening consideration of the future
should not be the province of the adolescent male only.
They belong to everyone --- everyone whose nose
has not yet been shaped to the curve of the grindstone
everyone who is yet undeceived
by the forms we've learned to inhabit.

We saw great changes in the world, and we wanted to know
What is happening and where is it going and what will it cost?
Will the future be a looping ride down a waterslide
or a bleak graveyard of hope
with escape just barely possible?

The future was a blank canvas,
painted light, or
painted dark, or
some mix thereof.

We asked:
what's it going to be?
We said:
stretch our minds
and give us some thrills while you're at it.

THE CREEK

Leopard frogs: sleek princelings of the amphibian world
      ballet dancer legs
          in spotted Renaissance tights
ready to spring fifteen feet if you get near them.
Plop! There he goes.

Crawdads, eyes on stalks
   peeping out of mudpile burrows.
Tiny black points of awareness.

Perch, hovering in the sunlit shallows
  in the hollow
    below the coiled barky roots.
A flick of the tail, and they're gone.
The water is brown & gold, like the stone called the Tiger's Eye.

Oarsmen beetles, dark little buttons
 row rapidly from the carpet of soggy leaves
to the surface, and just as rapidly back down.
On urgent missions.

Occasionally, we see
the hoary Godfather of them all
the snapping turtle
wide muscular clawed forearms
ridged back overgrown with moss
don't even try to pick this guy up.

The creek wanders along the ragged edge of town
through woods, then along the horse pastures
and hillsides that run to fields freshly bulldozed.
It disappears into culverts and becomes little but a roadside slough.
Development is on the way. Growth is forecast.

One must not strain after negligible effects. I don't really care what
happens to the creek. Like my grandparents, it made me what I am and
then it died. Life moves on, and life is change.
      Nevertheless
   it would be good

if kids everywhere
could leave playstations and x-boxes behind
to find a creek at the edge of town
where the thrashing crawfish in hand
and the sun-spotted embankment
might be savored
whose silence
could be posed against
the bustle of the mall
and win, like the Buddha, by doing nothing.

BICYCLE

Soft-drink bottle caps
   Nehi   Orange Crush   R.C.Cola
accumulated
   among the pebbles
at the foot of the wooden steps
     wherever a whitewashed store on cinderblocks
   lured us
with 'coke machine' out front
and wooden steps to sit on.

Inside, always   a wall calendar
a clock, lighted from the inside
frizzy-haired harridan   behind the counter
     gabby old men, in the chairs, talking about 'fishin'.
A candy bar, a moon pie, a small bag of peanuts:
   then back out   into the blazing day
     the withering heat:
we'd grasp the handlebars, and pedal out
   onto the shining streets again.

Every bicycle
   had a basket, mounted in front
     a wide, comfortable seat
     and a one-speed chain drive
that occasionally hopped off
   the toothed sprockets.
'Racing bikes'   were for rich kids
who loved form more than function
--- they didn't really ride them   all over town
like we did
they just kind of showed them to each other in the garage.

The bicycle   was our ticket
   Out Of The Home;
  we rode them   to one another's homes
   over the half-wooded hills
     to the municipal swimming pool, with towel and basketball
crammed into the front basket;
   to the newsstand, to buy some comix;

or over the jarring brick-cobbled streets of Old Town
   to find, perhaps, a little shop
      where a short dark man
with an air of sodden collapse about him
sold coins   dipping into the bucket
I could find nineteenth-century
   sous and kroner and pfennig
   or a worn Indian-head
and then out, on the streets again
   beneath the glorious blaze   the apocalyptic blast of afternoon
miles
      to a friend's house, to show him what I had found
  and then to play blackjack   for an hour
in the upstairs bedroom
   with pennies and dimes
   wasting the day   in an idler's pursuit
while his mother   ironed clothes   a floor below.

   Later   a few years later
      we rode   to the pool
to call the girls over to the fence
to tell one what someone had said
or to see where another would be going
   tonight
testing our dubious   power
      to make these compelling new-minted things
respond to us.

New-minted, they'd seized the power of sun and gold and all nature
tipped the table over
    usurped our universe
  all things previously valuable   now slid clattering to the floor.

Books, bikes, coins
  trips to the woods
 little critters   captured barehanded
    all slid clattering to oblivion
as we rose   and turned   to greet
the new goddess
     rising above the horizon:
   legs brown, gleaming
  shaking water from her hair.

(UNTITLED)

1

The past had swept in, and left pools of itself ---
    debris, flotsam ---
on the upcountry hillsides
around the tattered farmhouses
and along the lakefront
with its pontoon boat docks
and bait stores
and old men telling tales
of possum hunts and big fish.
It had cut roads deep
through the woods
and channels through the rocks
to right the roadways.

Certain neighborhoods were still moist with its redolence;
pungent with the summoning of memories
like the smell of unraked leaves after a rain.

The past might spring at you out of an attic trunk
opened, for the first time, after fifty years;
it might watch you, from a photograph of a hard-bitten face
with eyes inscrutable
a body dressed in somber black.

The past had washed up, leaving its water-line
along the hills, and the mossy rock walls
the brick-cobbled streets ---
washed up and subsided.
It had run back out, leaving relics, mysterious artifacts
in the empty upstairs bedrooms.
It left my grandparents sitting on their front porch.

It left the blue eagle of the National Recovery Act,
the web of home visits, skill trading and backyard gardening
that sprang up when the mighty had withdrawn behind their
moneyed clouds.

It left Mr. Roosevelt on the postage stamp
and, framed, on the back wall of the resale shop.

It left the taciturn men at feed store, whose knowledge was sealed
and incommunicable.

2

In the 1950's, a new life had arisen.
Summer had burst through the soil.
New day had broken, the world was good
and we were a part of it.
Love was ardent, and belief easy to come by:
easily solicited, and easily seduced.

3

The present hung its silver offerings
from the magazines and in the catalogs and the showrooms.
    Pick, and eat! was the message.
Wandering through the new garden, we sampled this and that
and found them to be good.

The Tree of Knowledge, though
when tapped
brought out the nightsticks and tear gas
and the dogs, maddened
whose eyes now unmasked shone with the light of hell
and who guard the gates, even today, snarling from the AM radio
straining to bite from behind their glassed booths.

4

My grandparents were incomprehending souls:
life had cut its flues through them, then subsided, leaving them
ghosts, drifting over the battlefield
or houses full of memories that made no sense ---
memories which still shed their light over the present
with the freshness of new moons.

They sat on their separate front porches, on opposite sides of town
and treated us with a fumbling kindness when we visited them, which was
often.

The present, though
had Elvis Presley on the radio
and the Five Satins
and Buddy Holly,
     Buddy Knox
      and <u>Ohh</u> --- <u>please</u> --- <u>stay</u> <u>by</u> <u>me</u>
                 <u>Diana</u>.
I couldn't resist it. Good was everywhere.

5

Out bicycling at nightfall
the crescent moon in the West, and Venus
I rode past the houses where whole lives were hidden
behind the yellow-lit windows
and the sweetness of life overcame me
& I longed to walk in
drink and eat in full
the wine and honey stored behind each yellow-lit window
know the truth
and shine with its knowledge.
Wind rushed past my face
and the first stars shone.

6

So who are you
to tell me, daily, from the radio and the TV
that I 'hate America', because I don't support your warlike projects?
That I'm 'bashing America', because I can
see the truth that's before my eyes?
Or that I'm a 'traitor', 'siding with our enemies'
because I'm not as wrong as you've consistently been?
      Part of growing up, I guess,
is finding out that the world is not entirely the place

one imagined it to be, and that flame-mouths
on furlough from hell
are a part of it.

                            7

In my pickup, I smuggle the good of the past
hidden beneath the floorboards, into the present
past the guards, and the dogs
and the television, and bling,
and all the Cool Stuff.
Here and there, in secluded nooks and picnics
or in the quiet eye, circled by the world's fray and fury
I unpack it to share with my companions
and a few children.

THE COUNTRY CLUB

The sandstone clubhouse
    sat fastened to the edge of the hills, or to a high plateau
    that fell rapidly away
to a valley below.

    The hillsides
  steep, and thickly wooded
   enjoyed a reprieve
a commutation
  (permanent, I hope)
    from the encroachments of the developers.

  The valley
a study in miniaturization
    and panorama
 could be seen
studied   admired
at leisure
   from the iron railing
 of the concrete deck
    behind the bar & kitchen.

Over the plateau, the golf course
 rolled away:
  small figures, walking
  a toy flag in every cup.

  My job
was to arrive at nine in the morning
   sweep up around the pool
    fetch and carry for whomever needed it
    then open the refreshment stand.
fifty yards away.

I had caddied at the golf course
over the past three summers
and the retiring fry cook
had recommended me.

At ten, the iceman would arrive
  in his truck
    hook a fifty-pound block with his tongs
      hoist it
        sling it along
          limping, from the war wound
            (someone told me)
      up the steps   drop the iceblock in the cooler
where I would chop it up.
Before the war, he'd delivered ice
      (he told me)
  in a horse-drawn wagon.

During the slow hours of the afternoon
  the cries from the pool drifted
   over the still air
   like birds' calls
     to me
as I sat
beneath the oak
  shading the foodstand
   and read J. G. Ballard and George Gamow:
     Terminal Beach and One Two Three Infinity
the valley spread out below me.
 No one cared
   that I was not on my feet
   so long as I cooked
     and kept the stand clean.
Eventually, a party of children
     would come up, towels slung round their hips
   and order.
The pubescent girls   would say foolish and daring things
   vying for the attention
of the Older Boy.

    One day, as I walked along the high deck   behind the bar
        a thunderstorm
which had been announcing its arrival   for an hour
   could be seen   thick low and heavy
hanging over the valley
   bright sunshine still to the right.

"C'mon in, it's going to rain," said the sometime golfer
sprawled on the deck chair; some intermediate stage of alcoholism
and sadness   and futile resistance to his own imminent extinction
visible in his jowls   and in the clouded, furtive eye.
   The ladies   at the nearby table   rose to do so.
   But he had been speaking to the children   of ten, eleven,
twelve   who stood, towel-wrapped, at the rail   looking out over the
spectacle   of a thunderstorm moving across the valley   from the
left   as the sun shone   on the lands   to the right.

   "C'mon in," he repeated
but they, leaning over the rail, did not hear him
or would not respond. At last, disgusted, he threw his napkin down
and joined the others   filing into the bar   the automatic door closed
behind them.

But the eight or nine children   of ten, eleven, and twelve
continued to watch
as the curtain of rain moved up the hill
and swept,
battering, over the clubhouse
   flinging a wet mist
      over their faces.

Later
I could not help but remember
      the kids who stood at that rail
   transfixed and astonished   by the winged dragon
moving through the sky
not that they were
 heroes of bratdom
   but their little maws were wide open
 hungry for grace and power
while their elder --- he wanted no more.

THE PLAIN & THE EXOTIC

1

Kitchen baking apron   Y'all come on in
a deliberate subjugation of the self to
plainness, modesty, simplicity;
nightly Bible readin's
a personality broad and flat as a pancake
--- near all the counties in the state voted 'dry'.
Nothin so good as home-baked bread.

In the lap of such determined ordinariness
all things not manageable
wither, dry up;
the wholesome, the necessary, and a drought of the spirit
pass one into the other ---
one is no longer distinguishable from the others.

The dark passions still break out:
jealousy, murder
just as in the old ballads;
but usually
after years of personal darkness
someone hangs himself in the barn.

Sixty years pass, everyone has moved to town;
life is dressed up
with chrome-plated geegaws
frilled out, but not deepened.
The elderly still scribble chapter & verse
talking about prophecy
and speculating on when God will come back to end it all.

2

The black-and-white photograph in the magazine:
  certainly the editors debated, and chuckled
    before deciding to send that one out
      to readers   in Middle America.

Two women who seem to be Italian
are walking down the cobbled pathway to the beach
 enveloped in a swarm-cloud of sensuality
  something has been brought to fruition in them
   fruition, and availability;
    Juno, Ceres
     presided over
      their making:
       lush beauty of
        their torsos
         spilling out:
        marble made flesh:
their Mediterranean eyes know me better than
                I know myself.

    What would my life be
     without this?
      Sensual conviction, or madness   overtook me.
       I must have this:
       I cannot settle for anything less.

Meanwhile, I mowed yards: trimmed around the rock circles
   enclosing the gardens: received my pay.
     Studied my schoolbooks;   passed the tests.

                3

Then, a year later, came a sound
from the jukebox
   jubilation in a great hollowringing cavern
    Gary Bonds and Daddy G
     the way he jumped on that song and dug in
      rode it joyfully
        like a big cat, teeth clamped on a zebra's back
       Doncha know that I danced   I danced!
        Till a quarter to three
            --- the people, who could be heard
             behind the lead vocal
          stomping, clapping, shouting, whooping, whistling
were getting messages from each others' flesh

                142

each body, a living transmitter & receiver
                --- I bought the record
        & lay with my head up against the speaker
                saying, praying
                take me, take me.
                I want to be where you are
                in that great hollow cavern
        with the fire leaping   from body to body:
                take me, I want to be there.

I KNOW WHAT YOU MEAN, BUT
WE'RE NOT LIKE THAT

Lives in the basement
  with his train set
    (nowadays, his computers);
Petrified by girls
Hopelessly klutzy
Makes stupid jokes that fall flat
Pencil neck, sloppy dresser.

Yes, we like science fiction, but we're
NOT LIKE THAT.
We're Regular Guys --- to you, anyway, buddy ---
with an extra dimension.
The Regular World   isn't quite enough.
We can't believe in it   wholeheartedly
or accept its well-meaning advice
but we will pursue its goals   provisionally.

Right now, we're trying to settle the dissention
   between family, church, and testosterone.
We're racked by the contradictions.
But keeping faith with everyone & everything
  is impossible.
Something's got to give.

Come summer, we'll play basketball 5 or 6 hours a day
  when not working.

Go to the lake, sit on the hood of the car,
& consider the future.

On the court, the sun roasts my shoulders till they prickle.

I've got a regular girlfriend
like a responsible guy should have
but still my heart strays off
to the beaming honey, all cheeky grin
& utter thoughtlessness
pure American pie.

IN THE TOWN

1

Newspaper pages
    covered with line-drawn illustrations
    of men in suits
        shaded gray.

Special! Sale!

Batteries and windshield wipers
    at the auto parts.

Slick color pages in the news mag:
    Schenley and Courvoisier
        by a fireside.

All things to clothe the outside of life
    and make it tolerable.

As children, we lived in a kind of interregnum
    between one dispensation, and the next.
        Between the Farm World
            the Town World
            and the Great World.

Like a spring tornado, the rake of economic fact
had passed over the countryside
dragging the insufficiently rooted into town
where they would await   the next dispensation
the next orders from God.

The town had its thriving businesses   its struggling businesses
and the poorly fenced neighborhoods of the less fortunate
'across the tracks' or 'down by the river' or 'on the east side':
neighborhoods where dogs lay in the streets in insolent laziness
and children ran barefoot.
Newspapers blew up against rusty wire fences and hung there like
lost souls.

The crash and splinter of breaking glass could be heard, in the vacant
lots.
So unlike the neighborhoods in the better part of town
with their one-acre lawns and spearpoint iron fences;
with books in the study, and, outside, the statuary drowsing
in the long Edwardian afternoon. Some afternoons
a party might be decreed for the children: a babble of color, amidst
the greenery.

If there was a 'plant', its whistle blew at noon
and again at the end of the day
when men walked out of its gates.

Here in the town could be heard the distant echoes --- a faint clangor,
rolling across the plains --- the hammer-blows of a new world forming
a colossus formed by men themselves
engineering pressed steel   chemicals   electricity
and relying on sales power.

2

We were in between all things. What remained of the farm was:
   the snowy-browed old man, framed, on the wall, with his Civil
War whiskers;
   the farm implements in the toolshed
   Grandfather, in his sling-chair on the front verandah
   reading Progressive Farmer magazine
   ice-water by his side
   the potato cellar, the canning rituals
   great-aunts in the country, visited in the summer
and the characters of the grandparents, formed in the 1800's, subsisting,
somewhat uselessly, on the coattails of today. Their characters said: tend
to all things. Do right.

Sometimes, on the radio, we heard the music of the old-time people:
a thin wail, a guitar, and a fiddle. In my private mind, I called it,
the Songs of Malnutrition.

Cars ruled the streets of Today. Suited men with shiny hair slicked back
spread their hands and introduced us to the Kitchen of Tomorrow.

Housewives fondled refrigerators and cooking ranges in the
magazines' ad pages.
A youthful attitude and appearance were striven for.
Out with the Old!
Soon, we would grow big enough
to take our place buying and consuming. In the meantime,
before we signed our name on the line and became Responsible,
briefly, we were Free: children. It was the interregnum.

Still, the shape of an earlier, more stringent time might be glimpsed
through the Sunday stillness of today:
it hovered, barely concealed, in the family background, like the deep-
striking tones
of the Grandfather clock, whose gonglike <u>bong</u>
was instantly recognizable through the house
in daylight or in darkness.
It hovered like the ghost of that tone, still resonant on the air.

Yet, despite --- or amid --- the refrigerators, the new cars, the slick
magazines, despite (or amid) the new money and the old, we felt the
concealed forces, like whales, moving beneath the surface, stirring the
waters.

Unlike Ahab, who wrecked himself senselessly, I had friendly feelings
for the whale, and when he trumpeted I swam out to join him.

I had happy visions that made no sense. I saw the whale breaching,
rolling, high over the town, in the long summer afternoons; I saw myself
as a gull, or an air swimmer, his companion or herald, through the long
golden days. As a lark, I wrote my imaginings in a paper and handed it
in, half-joking, as an assignment. The priest read it, and --- what else
did I expect? --- tore it up, looking straight at me, without a word.

Sure, I had gone off the rails on that one.

(WORKING TITLE: MY NECK OB DE WOODS)

1

The mountains
  lay like a woman in irregular slumber
      (knee up, half on her side)
      beneath a drawn spread
        of endless green.

Her angularities had been softened, smoothed
  by forty million years of rainfall;
   sharpness worn away
    by the water which cut, rushing,
     through the passes
      rounded all edges
       and pooled up in the valleys
        in great glassy lakes
         to which the Indians gave names.

A smoky haze
  drifted over the higher parts.

The animals
  were the usual North American cast of characters:
    deer, bear, quail, and turkey;
      streams full of perch, bass, and turtles;
       cottonmouth hid in the shallows.

It was a hunter's paradise.

2

Two, three hundred miles away
   the big wide river
    looped and meandered southward.
  Its white breath   covered the lowlands   each night
with a mist
  that was burned away each morning   by the orange sun.
  Its flooding

its rise and fall
   had carried the silt from the highlands, and spread it
   over the lowlands, and enriched them;
   so here the farming tribes
  (married to Sister Corn)
had settled and raised their corn and squash, and built
their huge earthen mounds
 till the diseases came.

         Then the land went back   to the wild things.
         Grass grew, then shrubs   in the village commons
            and insects infested the thatched roofs
                and the rafters collapsed.

Then the peace of morning
lay over the land like a dream once again.
Sorrow expired with the last human consciousness
and no one knows where souls go ---
if indeed they go anywhere ---
other than back to the source:
the shining river, the low mist,
the orange sun
and the dream.

                    3

The first men from Europe
who came to the hardwood forests
to the mountains, the waterfalls, and the lakes
were big, yawping backwoods men
exulting in the freedom of new escape.
They spread their arms wide
and told tall tales.
They hunted the bear and the deer.
They fought the Indians
and married among them.

The next men to come from Europe
were the men of the coin
looking for new prospects.
They saw the wide flat river deltas

and knew just what to do with them.
Wielding the coin, they hired the sword to capture slaves
and bring them to the river bottoms
and make them raise cotton, and harvest it.
Europe needed new clothes.

While these strong and foresightful men took the rich lands
the little men, fleeing these men and their world
the little men, who'd left
bondage and confinement
the backwoods farmers
foolhardy, striking out on their own
knowing only land and family
filtered in from the east
carrying rifles and seeds and axes,
crockery and a family bible
speaking the loose-limbed broken-springed
language of hain't and arter;
they came, and took their lodging
in the crannies of the wooded hills.

For a time they were left alone
to plow their little patches
to patch their leaking roofs
to butcher the hogs, and hang them in the smokehouse
and to fiddle on the front porch, or in the barn
as the more agile swung about.

The Indians did not all die:
some still lived
in the south, and in the west
so the Great White Father
conducted some forceful negotiations
and induced them to move
to the Indian Territory.

Laura Ingalls saw them lined up, on their ponies.
An Indian baby looked at her, straight into her brain, and
she called to her father to let her keep that baby,
but the horses moved on, and she threw a fit.

Her pa was a fiddler, too.

The railroads slung their steel webs
across the Great Plains
and finally came to Arkansas   and then produce
was no longer sent by boat
down the river, but was brought to town, and loaded on boxcars, and sent
overland
at fifty, sixty, seventy, eighty
ninety miles an hour.
From the web of railroads, millionaires arose: beef millionaires
pig millionaires   rail millionaires   steel millionaires   grain millionaires
shipping millionaires.
Wealth shone its brassy light
through the land, and through the minds
of the people   who looked on.
While many feared the new influence
of this 800-pound gorilla
that bought congressmen, that changed laws or
broke them with impunity
many others were awed, and thought
I want to get me some of that.
Books were written
about wealth, and how to get it.
If you didn't avail yourself of opportunity,
you were a laggard   dumb, or just not wide-awake.
Wealth was proof of diligence
intelligence
proof of persistence
of a bright attitude the right attitude.
If you weren't wealthy, then you lacked diligence
or smarts or the right attitude.
These three together constituted virtue, in the new world
of opportunity.

Arkansas hung back, but the gospel of wealth
did have its influence
in every town.
Books extolling Jesus

as "the greatest salesman of them all"
sold.
You had but to "think and grow rich."
Uneasy, illicit hybrids
of wealth's gospel, and Jesus'
were born.
(Though there was precious little of this wealth around.)
A New Man, with faith in the future
shaking hands, and radiating optimism
made himself, stood on his own two feet
and walked down Main Street.

PREFACE

Handed down from feudal times,
preserved in dukes' libraries, or in monks'
we have woodcuts showing
peasants' life by the month:
bearded men with blank eyes
& scarved helpmates
breaking the soil with oxen
seeding from shoulder-slung bag
hoe and scythe and scare-crow and knife
slaughter of pigs and so on --- the life unchanged
for fifteen hundred years
since the Romans.

America, though, flew on winged feet ---
ripped through the wilderness, cleared forests, built roads
sent steamboats up and down the river
dug out the ores
kept an eager eye on the bank account.
Nevertheless, certain seasons of peace
of catch-up
of easy breathing and good feeling
emerged up here and there when breakneck change stood still
and gains were consolidated.

To children, then, it seemed that life
had something of the eternal about it; the small town and the farm
drifted upward to
an apotheosis with the divine
merged with the heavens
and might have had constellations named after
their mundane but transfigured features: the plow, the bridle, the parlor
piano
or the corner store, the television antenna, and the bicycle.
Orion might have become Davy Crockett
and Sagittarius, the Apache
or the terrible Comanche
now lifted to heaven in starry configuration.

It was then, in these seasons of peace and perfection
that the Dance of the Seasons might be cut again, in wood,
or touched, in bright ink, to decorate the chapter heads
of an illuminated manuscript.
With this in mind, I wrote
this half-year of commemoration.

MARCH

Eventually winter falls to a guerilla war of attrition.

Unseasonable bouts of warmth gather
and infiltrate the uplands
drifting in when no one expects them, in the dead of night.
They seize key posts and hold entire towns hostage for days before
they're forced back by a furious counterattack from the north.
But in the meantime, the insurgents
have won the hearts & minds of the townsmen.
People shed coats, marvel at the weather,
walk in fields made glorious by
the free gold pouring from the sky.
The north has not yet done its worst; now it sends gloom, cold rain,
windstorms, tornadoes. But it's too late. People secretly wait for the
rebels' next advance, and for the true king to return.

APRIL

Kites ride in the wind:
Paper sewn on a flimsy stick cross
tugs like a sky fish
pulls & dives, then gathers strength to
swim like a proud sailfin
in the blue.

MAY

It's almost here.

School draws us in, as always, through its stone arched mouth
and expels us seven hours later, reduced to lethargy
but now insubordination is dancing in our bodies
secrets are whispered

& laughter suppressed.
We may comply but we don't care.

The water has risen
and is cutting away at the caked sand.

The blackrobes can hiss about obedience, but
in a few weeks they will fall aside like burned paper
banished by the dew
whisked back to their convents where they will
inflict their renunciations on each other, but not on us.
Their rule is ended.

The benevolent sun has returned
    to save his children
& gather them up into his lap.
Soon he will lock the schoolhouse doors, and say,
Leave this place, and see the world I have prepared for you.
See how I have infused it with life, the same life
that fills you and begs you to run free, to
climb trees and skin your knees.
Stretch up in gratitude, and celebrate;
join me for the three long months ahead.

JUNE, JULY, AND AUGUST

Children run back and forth through the whirling water arcs
spun off by the lawn sprinklers
Whee!
Across the street, the neighbor girl, in her knit pink swimsuit
proud & gawky in new womanhood
locks her thighs across the saddle
and canters her horse across the yard & clops on down the street
her sun-bleached hair a crown, but
the giant beast seems barely under her control.
At the lake
dogs swim from boat to shore and stand on the sand shaking off
sun glares wobbling off the green lake water

as the boat rocks hypnotically.
Why do I have to wear this life preserver? I can swim!

> It's summertime, summertime, sum- sum- summertime
> Summertime!
>> --- The Jamies

> June, July, and August:
> June, July, and August
> Gonna shout
> School's out!
> That's when the good times roll!
>> --- sung by Freddy Cannon

At the drive-in, boys lounge sprawling in giant cars the size of boats
and spend what little money they have
to catch the attention of the girls, six to a car

> Lord, I've got to raise a fuss
> Lord, I've got to raise a holler
> About working all summer
> Just to try and earn a dollar.
>> --- Eddie Cochran

At the pool, the short brown lifeguard
built to astonish
celebrates his bold new command of movement
by bouncing all his weight off the diving board
and soaring free in a high arc
becoming, for that moment, a gull in flight
glorious, a hero of the afternoon.

Not far away, boys mob the concrete
beneath the basketball goal.
Unfettered at last, they collide en masse as
the ball booms off the metal backboard
or shoots off-court in a missed pass.
When they've played to exhaustion, they abandon the court
and plunge into the swimming-pool, into
oblivion, as
cold sensation erases all else.

"Come with me to the park, we'll hit some balls."
Steve, Bill, Jane, Bill's little brother and I mount our bicycles
and pump to the blazing green field.
It seems
that a sleek white-pelted animal is buried between my shoulders
as I take the bat, roll from side to side
and begin to pop flies
each into the intended glove.
I may be slow, sometimes inept, but
<u>this</u> one thing I can do just right.
I'm in the groove.
Soon, I'll have to let someone else have the fun, but now
my heart and spirit soar with the tumbling ball
as I watch its high summertime arc.

When we're all hot and sweat-soaked, there's red soda pop
at the store. The smooth ring of glass
rolls along my lips, then the cold red drenches my tongue. Yum!

Evening floats down over the world
like a scarf
softening the bright edges of day.
Giant moths and hummingbirds
buzz and fumble at the blossoms
as we sit, watching, in the lawn chairs
and bats flap and swoop on their nightly patrols.
The Summer Triangle --- Deneb, Vega, Altair --- begins to shine
above
and the giant fishhook Scorpio fills the South.
From the damp places, little frogs shrill; while,
beneath the porch light, the old toad waits for insects to fall,
stunned by the hot globe.

A BOY'S DILEMMA

"Man, she doesn't know why you're not talking to her. 'He's sitting with
<u>that girl</u>,' she says."
      We are at the State Park, at the lodge pool, where, across the
flagstones, I've seen the goddess to end all goddesses, the radiant

sculptured sun-browned daughter of new wealth who thinks the world is hers. I don't dare talk to her. Instead, I'll talk to anyone else. At her table she looks angry and frustrated, and I know I'm lookin' good, but I also know I don't have what it takes to engage this daughter of Plutus, and she'll find this out if we talk for about ninety seconds. So it's best we just circle each other like twinned planets, never to collide.

To my left, my new acquaintance is talking about the girl he met yesterday. "So I went to her room after midnight and knocked real soft, and she opens it a little and says, 'They're asleep --- ' "

But I'm only half interested in his story and not at all in the perfectly nice girl I've been sitting with. All I can see is the glorious hair of the princess. She floods the air with a sensuality that has never known doubt or repression. She is utterly confident, and that's why she needs the King of All Jocks, not some bookish devotee of J.G. Ballard who's only minimally athletic but looks like he's more than he is.

But what can you do when all your senses have been mobilized and you're pointing like a bird dog?

BRUTE RHAPSODY

They're really rockin' in Boston
Pittsburgh, PA
Deep in the heart of Texas
Around the Frisco Bay
Way out in St. Louie
And down in New Orleans ---

--- Chuck Berry

Kids from one end of the country to the other are hooked into an electric
union: they're aware of each other and themselves --- conscious of their
physical powers & their open futures as no previous generation had
been. Money, sports and good looks rule their world, and alcohol is
the new adventure; heedless optimism fills their songs, State U is their
destination, and Daddy's new gift of a car will drive them there.

Boys lost in giant suburban homes are playing surf guitar in their
bedrooms, while pampered heartbreakers, experts in eyeliner, are ready
to take over the sororities at State U and State Tech. The summer elicits
dreams of breaking loose --- a convertible with its top down is forever
pulling away from wherever-it-may-be to seek a better destination across
town or down the highway.

We're free and nothing will stop us!

Or, as a later generation put it, "We're the kids in America!"

MY LAWN-MOWING EMPIRE

1

Streaks of shadow lay across every lawn;
necklaces of dew
hung by spiders, working overnight
glistened with dawn.
Slick abundances of grass, riotous and unshorn, flashed in the sun,
not knowing what kind of haircut was in store for them.

2

The gasoline mower bumped and rattled
& jarred my shoulders
as I pushed it from our garage
down the driveway and
over the streets
to the lawn du jour.
Positioning it at the yard's margin,
I kicked aside the asphalt cakes, braced my foot against the case
and pulled back on the starter-rope.
The motor choked and stuttered
and announced itself to the world.
Birds fled alarming to the trees.
Squirrels tumbled over each other to race up the trunks.
A brattling noise of aggression filled the air.

      I was the operator of the Machine
destroyer of the silence. It was as loud as a motorcycle, but useful,
and therefore
justifiable. It flung its echoes back from all sides.

3

The grass stood in angry resistant clumps, spears upraised.
It would not go down easily.
Sometimes I had to butt at it like a bull, or drive the mower forward
like a sled.

I rammed it over the clumps of nutgrass, then bogged down
in gopher holes; jerked it around corners, and edged carefully along
the gardens.
From the port, a chopped lawn salad sprayed out in an airborne
arc: sharp grassy oils and spices mingled with puffs of half-burned
hydrocarbons.
When I pushed too forcibly and the mower over-gorged and died, I bent
over it to spit on the muffler
and watch the foam boil off in seconds.

As the morning wore on, the sweat stood so thick on my brow I would
be licking salt water off my lip as it dripped. If I were working at an
older lady's house, she might have an iced cola waiting for me, a reward
for valor. I would sit on her porch, letting the breeze cool me for a
moment. We might talk.

"You seem to work so hard at this. How many lawns do you take
care of?"

"I have five right now, ma'am."

"Would you like another?"

"Yes ma'am, I would. Do you know someone?"

"Let me call my daughter."

"How big is her lawn?"

"Oh, it's bigger than mine. But she lives on 20th Street."

"That's all right."

"You know, when Lanie was still at home --- Lanie's my little
girl --- she and your mother used to go to class together. Both of them
sang in glee club. The school put on a stage show one year, and your
mother played in the band. She was a very good musician. She played
for all the weddings and Christmas and Easter mass."

"Uh."

"Before they got married. But that seems like only yesterday."
Silence.

Finally she might ask me something about my plans. What was
I going to do with myself? I didn't know: I had no plans. I could not
imagine the future and was not eager for it to arrive.

4

At the end of a half-day, after I'd trimmed and raked, I would
present myself to receive my pay. I might sit in her kitchen and note the
bric-a-brac upon the shelves, the painted statuettes, the photos of people

whose faces had been formed by the stresses and limitations of an earlier era, whose clothing was more somber than any I saw now. Six dollars and fifty cents was good pay; ten dollars was a fortune. She might linger over my company, but never anything so blatant as Blanche Dubois who kissed the young man. I would tell her I would be back in a week, or in two weeks. Then I would push the mower home, bouncing it over the streets.

5

Older people were formed by the Past, and they still lived in it, but the middle-aged businesspeople lived in the Now, which they owned and operated. I mowed some of their lawns, too. Their kitchens might have an island in the center, with stovetop and stone countertops and a flared copper hood above. Preoccupied, they paid me and went back to their bustle, unloading the car or wrangling the children. They had seized the moment and were wrestling it to earth. The present and the future were theirs. They knew where they were going and what they were doing. The old people were pleasant, but they were from another world, and that world was falling apart or graying under a rain of dust or being sold off piece by piece.

Always, the future waited: empty, demanding. What was I going to be? The lady had asked me but I could not answer.

6

With the money from mowing, I bought ice cream and trips to the pool and paperback books and occasionally I would waste it on a pinball machine. Or I would sit around a table with my friends and gamble at poker and blackjack. In a year or two I would discover 45 rpm records, and soon I would haunt the record stores, agonized with an extravagant new hunger and looking longingly at the album covers. I quickly memorized a hundred lyrics, and became an ardent apostle for rock 'n' roll.

In my books I'd read about the heroic paleontologists, Marsh and Cope and Andrews, but recovering dinosaur bones did not seem to me to be a realistic career choice. My head was filled, too, with pictures of caves, from The National Geographic Magazine, corridors of flowstone and nests of crystal and huge humped pillars, so exploring caves seemed to be a wonderful thing to do, but this was no real career either.

One night my father took me for a drive; his job took him to many of the small towns in our area. I think he too wanted to know what I was going to do with myself. I was always a bit strange to him, a mystery. He was shaped by the Depression and then by the Army. Responsibility had weighed down on him early. I had my chores to do but no responsibility, for no one depended upon my income. In place of responsibility, then, I indulged my enthusiasms, few of which he shared. Poker, yes; caves, no. Stamp collecting, yes --- he had passed his collection on to me. Rock 'n' roll, no.

He asked me what I was most interested in. The trees sped by outside the car, and the starry night hung behind in the great unmoving.

I said that I was most interested in the music I heard on the radio, for that was the case at the time, and I went on to claim, with little knowledge, that songwriting was better now than it had ever been. To illustrate, I sang a few verses of I Can't Help It If I'm Still In Love With You.

This must not have been too good an omen, because talk moved on to other areas. I told him that chemical rockets were really not so good for interplanetary travel, but something I'd been reading about called the ion engine promised to be much better.

"Oh," he said, "I see. Your mind's out there."

He spoke with the skepticism of James Garner: friendly, reeling sideways.

"Yes," I asserted. "That's what's going to be happening."

He had met with reality and it had focused him. I was older than a child but I still lived in the world of dream and open possibility. Postwar prosperity had buffered so many of us: no one, so far as I knew, lived in need. Such was the world that I did not leave behind for quite a while.

My father made the occasional attempt to understand me on my own terms, if he could discover what these were. He was not musically inclined, so he ceded this part of me to my mother, who was. Much else of what I did seemed strange to him. My mother had a censor's interest in my reading habits, and often the line of worry creased her brow whenever she suspected that the books I read were carrying me further from Holy Mother Church, in Whom and only in Whom true salvation was to be found. Possibly at her prodding, my father asked to see some samples of what I was reading. He liked 'The Big Black and White Game' and 'The Quaker Cannon', but found the rest insubstantial. Probably his report to her was, It's harmless, because she bothered me no more, although worry was always visible in her gaze.

Occasionally during the summer I would climb up in one of the trees in my grandfather's orchard, with a book, trying to cram all the sensations of living --- the bright green, the morning air, the odor of ripe fruit --- into my nervous system, while simultaneously being excited by a book. Or I might sit on the roof of his tool-shed, trying to do the same. But the pleasures of the real world and those of the imagination were incompatible, and could not be captured at the same time. If I read "Dark Universe" or "A Scent of Sarsaparilla" the fireworks went off in my head no matter where I was --- and when I pushed the mower through the wet grass and the sliced stalks released their prickly nose-tease and the salt sweat ran down my face, the heat and the roar of the engine embroiled me in a bath of sensation too virile to need the help of the imagination.

In a year I had found a job fry cooking and I walked away from my lawn-mowing empire, leaving it, I suppose, to some leathery old black man or scrambling go-getter like myself. The future was out there, still waiting, but I continued to duck away from it, evading all choices. Teachers and parents, all expected me to leap from the familiar to the unknown, guided by some immature vision of a future finished self --- a self embodied in an occupation --- but the only current that bore me forward was my passion for rock 'n' roll, and this, like cave exploring or bone hunting, offered me no conceivable work with a future. To oblige the grownups, though, I cobbled together some career plans, based on my skills: math and science. Everyone approved, but the plans were hollow, and they splintered at the first blow.

END OF EMPIRE

No stelae carved with recumbent dandelions
oozing, decapitated
would be found beneath the rose-bushes
to celebrate my whirling blades of victory
the bull-like invincibility of my war-engine
or the godly patronage of my reign.

No clay tablets, ruled, would count the clinking silver
of the homeowners' tribute.
Like stone-headed Ozymandias and his over-reach,
my empire would fade from every human memory.

Only I remain, to mark the papyrus
or indent the clay
to tell the reader
the glory that was.

Mark my words, passer-by!
Life is fleeting!
Even the prick in warm pussy
will be but a memory
as evanescent as yesterday's clouds
or withered as last summer's leaves.

Therefore I entreat ye: listen to my wisdom
imparted in books to come;
buy every one, and be on watch
for the salient words I shall drop.

4: Odds and Ends

I could see the Tao
in the ethereal finesse of
certain of the elderly.

Now that all was spent and done,
mind had drifted free
and hovered above them
like fine silvery smoke.

They were like panes of glass
and, looking through, I could see
a pulsing
then, the jumbled hardware of yesterday
and finally, a will-to-good still seeking
to thread itself through the world.

These were my great-aunts, great-uncles
and grandparents.

I studied their books and pamphlets ---
a bound copy of Edgar A. Guest and his lamentable poems
woodcuts printed on frail paper
furniture, thick-boned in the semi-darkness
a dish of arrowheads, picked up on the farm.

My mother asked, "Are you going to become
an antiquarian?"

I wanted to soak, to revel
in the past.
I wanted to know
where it had all come from.
I became a guest to
haunted empty rooms
from which life had withdrawn;
guest to
the warm well-lit bedrooms
the kitchens, and
the summer's front porch
where the vine had knotted its huge woody trunk
tying earth & itself to the trellis.

I mowed their yards, sweating oceans in the sun.
As my physical powers increased,
a world opened up before me
in all its brightness, while theirs declined, but
the brightness drew me forward.
Still, the past exerted its influence, and
I was a creature of two worlds.

1931: CLUES IN THE AIR

Odors filled the air of the 'hood like invisible sponge-cake. The bracing scent of barley poured from an open window when someone was brewing beer; it rolled on down the street and by lifting their noses boys could figure out who was filling the tub and defying the government's Prohibition. And when Lent came, barrels of kippered herring were set out on the back porch; the sharp tang of salt fish signaled the season of fasting and repentance, and the neighborhood smelled like a Brooklyn corner grocery.

Most families kept backyard chickens. Chickens lent a sour and raffish smell to the alleyways behind the yards ---

--- and from there the piece slid into cuteness, chicken jokes and sanctimonious nostalgia and I can't seem to comb the crap out of it. Some good lines, yes, but the rest is dreadful. Abolish!

Well, of course we want to save a little. Just to show you the general arc.

"Come the fall, tomato bushes were uprooted and flung into a pile; tie-stakes were pulled and stacked next to them. Leaves raked away from the fences were set ablaze, and the bushes thrown on top; then the ashes were mixed with chicken droppings and spread over the bare furrows of the vegetable gardens. Rainfall would do its job, white fungi would spread its webs --"

. . . and the closer, very pagan.

"Women knelt on the black earth to set out their seedlings ---"

The streets were cobbled in red brick:
a bumpy ride for a boy on a bicycle.

The sidewalks were no better, for the erupting roots
had cracked the plates, tilting them ---
& made for broken-field running if you were on foot.
But I savored these things, for these were signs
of the venerable, the established
my fortress against modernity, against
the yellow-lined strip asphalt and the
endless parking lot.

COLD WAR VIGNETTE

The trees break out in bloom
& the clover covers the hillsides
and we cannot wait to throw aside our books
to lay & roll in the clover
breathe in its sweet pollen
to waken those dormant cavities
behind the nose
return home all itchy and grassy.

In school, we'd seen the spinning world globe
and learned   that
God's finger   had sliced through the clouds
and touched America
and filled it with His blessing.

As children
raised in the glow of the kitchen-morning sun
fed tales   with sliced bananas in milk
we came to believe that the clear and unobstructed light
of the new day
which streamed in over the eastern hills
before we left for school
was ours to give   to the rest of the world
we came to believe
that we had a wonderful way   to show the world.
We were not certain what our wonderful way was, but
we knew the world needed it
for the world lacked   all that we had.

The world was in need of   our loaded breakfast table
of   our orderly lives
our motor-cars   our tidy homes
our modest churches   wherein was found   a Better Way.
The world was in need of   our very Americanness
and we --- we were the very ones to dispense it to them.

But --- the trouble was ---
the world was so often ungrateful

when we came   to help them out
to show them the way
or to straighten them out.

Wickedly ungrateful --- it flung our proffered help
back in our faces
told us to get out   go home!

Well!
Just look at the mess they were in   without us!

We knew there were good people, responsible people
among them
who earnestly begged us to stay.
We heard about these people so often.
But we could not ignore
the mobs who pelted our officials with stones
or the monks who burned themselves.

There had to be something else at work here.
Some cosmic anti-wonderfulness principle.
Some inversion of all that was good and holy.
Something opposed to All We Stood For.
Something created by the Devil himself
to thwart us.

PAPER RUN

Our paper boy had been called away for two weeks in December, and somehow I'd been picked to take over his route.

I think my parents figured it would be good for me. Give the boy a little responsibility. My mother's picture of the world was compounded of Norman Rockwell's paper-boys and Bing Crosby's priests; and my father always remembered his first jobs.

I had to fold the papers the night before. Back then a newspaper was folded into a square, four sections over and three across, making it the right size & shape to be flung over a hedge or a fence or a car. Sail and float and plop down. I had fifty-something papers to fold, late at night, and I couldn't do it. I was too slow. My father had to join in.

I was up at 5 AM. The bag was slung over my bicycle. I'd had no practice run. I had a hand-drawn map with houses marked with X's.

The morning was dark and chill --- something like twenty-five degrees. Wobbling to the end of the drive, I dug in and pumped like a racer. Ice wind stung my cheeks, my fingers went numb, but intrepidity was my watchword. Even with a map, though, my head was soon a-whirl. Was that house on the left before or after the one on the right? The X's were not exactly clear. Rushing downhill, I had no way, and actually no desire, to stop to park and clarify matters. And that paper hung in the top of the 12-foot hedge --- was I to get off my bike and try to knock it out of the branches? I was afraid I was screwing up, but there was no time for a re-do. I had to get back home, eat breakfast, and leave for school.

Soon after, the calls began coming in. When I returned, my mother was in a state, as they say. So many people had not gotten their paper, but I had thrown them all. There was no way to rectify.

The next day it was the same.

Within a week they had found someone to replace me.

185

Nothing further was said. A great and profound silence enveloped the topic. Everyone felt that discretion was the wisest course. The boy will have to find some other way to prove himself. Time heals.

Not true, I found --- shame never dies. Shame rises around you like a thick cloud, a hot mist, a bath of failure. Perhaps I should have sought help in confession, but the church was more preoccupied with quashing the desires of the flesh, for which I felt guilt, but no shame. The need to meet expectations was the defining theme of our generation; the failure to do so its defining trauma. Failure prowled like a hungry cat in the bushes. We would do anything to avoid that. Our job was to carry the flag against Russia, plant it on higher ground --- make America proud. The marines at Iwo Jima were our icon.

DAD'S OLD BUD

I met Gene in later years; this time I was the comic dupe. I was just
out of my teens, home from college and blazing with adoration for
Huey Newton, who I thought was God's Second Coming and Greatest
Gift to Mankind. Gene came by the house one day to talk, I suppose,
about old times. I'd never met him before. In his button-up sweater
and smooth mustache, he might have been Cleveland on 'Family Guy':
a little overweight, settled into middle age, a satisfied man. The Post
Office had done him good. He and my father watched me with sly
amusement --- my father had undoubtedly warned Gene about my
radical enthusiasms. I knew not what to say. Steeped in a world of
revolutionary fury, ardor and brinksmanship, I quickly discovered I
was a creature of fantasy next to their sober reality. I could say little
or nothing beyond the elementary pleasantries. Like two old cats with
deep eyes, they watched me stumble and try to unite my mental life
with the reality before me --- two old cats, settled down and grown
substantial. They let me off easy, with the tolerant smiles of experience
for the young and extra-passionate.

INTERRUPTED

At the store, an old woman caught at my sister's sleeve. "You're Susan Westphal, aren't you," she announced --- her voice in all its hoarse certainty might have come from the Cave of the Sybil. My sister confirmed her identity.

"Your father was the best baseball player anyone had ever seen." Excited but halting, her voice ran on past all obstacles. "We watched him play shortstop, and my father said he was the best, and my brothers too. The Cardinals sent a man down to talk to him about one of their teams." Like an ancient marineress, she would not let go. She meant the St. Louis Cardinals' farm teams.

And did he sign?

"Yes, he sure did."

Then why didn't he play?
Well, that's the rest of the story.

Weeks before he'd have left, he'd gone on a hunting trip with three of his friends; they drove deep into Oklahoma, up and down through the blasted cuts in the folded rock with a lonely fringe of trees high above. Then, suddenly, the classic situation --- on a long slope, the brakes were gone.

Uncontrolled, the car rushed down the hillside as the boys shouted and braced for impact. Then the curve --- the car left the highway and turned over, and rolled. All the boys lived, but when my father crawled out and stood on the highway he found his sleeve filling with blood. His left arm had been caught outside the car in one of its rolls.

Another driver found them and took them on to a hospital, along with their guns, but my father's arm was unsalvageable. He refused to have it amputated. It swelled up, turned black, but nature took a strong hold and saved him from maiming --- at a price: he was a ballplayer no more. The arm would not fully extend.

"When he met me," my mother said, "he told me that was all over now."

Certainly the Cardinals' legal department voided his contract for non-fulfillment. At best, a quiet, gray-haired man came down from St. Louis, shook his head, and wrote a small check. Maybe there was a flash of sadness --- thought we had a good one there, kid --- a handshake, good luck to you, then my father was back in the neighborhood looking for a new future.

Had it not been for the old woman, we'd never have known.

A THRIVING BURG

1

It was more than a town;
it was a town with prospects
a town whose growth had never been slowed or stalled.

The old money
had enshrined itself
in colonnaded houses
behind acres of lawn
well-kept shrubbery & ancient trees.

The new money
(from automobiles and liquor
and real estate, and construction)
had flown to
the white homes in the hills
south of town
and nested.

The factories --- not too many, and not too big ---
served the town through hard times and
hired many a man in good.
They underwrote prosperity,
and sometimes pumped money with a vengeance.
At noon, and at five o'clock,
all the whistles blew.

Outside town, the fields swept in:
pleated rows that stretched from the highway to the horizon
divided by
fingers of woods along the rivers
& streambeds
that passed, in all their frontier beauty,
beneath the overpasses
stony and alluring, even though boys no longer went there
to fish or to swim.

But mostly, there were the old houses
in the old style
and the new houses
in a modern style.
WWII was the great divider.

2

The people, too were
a mix of old style and new style.
There were country people
cut loose by falling prices and high payments:
people who saw no future.
They came to the town to learn new ways
but old memories hung over them
like willow over the riverbank.

There were businesspeople, who had made the town
first by provisioning wagon trains
then by cutting the forests, and now
with outside investments
and showrooms and brochures and a hotel or two.
They knew the future lay in the flow
of bills over the counter
and orders placed from afar.

There were the brown-skinned people
impenetrable in their hidden knowledge.

There were the Germans,

and the Italians, and the Irish:
all devout candle-lighters.

There were other churches
that made a religion of solid prosperity
or of doctrinal purity ---
the proper method of baptism, or
the finer points of Resurrection Day ---
but all bristled with vigilance against the un-American:
the Eastern liberal and the Roman Catholic.

3

Men liked to fish   and shoot
and listen to the radio. Bait stores
lined the highway, and many would hitch the boat to the truck on
Saturdays. Or else, they would unfold the sling chairs in the back yard
and switch on the radio and open the beer cans and sit, intent on the St.
Louis Cardinals, sipping Busch. Their moans and cheers rose in unison,
in answer to the excited solo of 'Harry Carey'.
   "That boy, I don't think he can hit the fast ball."
   "How you know that, Arthur?"
   "I seen him when I went to St. Louis."

4

Sundays: tablecloths were spread
and fried chicken was served
with potatoes and gravy.
Children pulled off their starched shirts
and hurried to eat, then to play.

5

Adult intentions held the town together and kept it running on the
rails, bound for glory. Belief and striving --- that was the ticket. The
few who had fallen away --- through drink, or sloth, or broken-
heartedness --- were to be pitied for the sake of their children. They
watched, with sullen dark looks, as the train huffed and pulled away. It
was a shame, a damn shame. But the United States was a powerful
engine and soon everyone would be drawn forward, hooked to its
ingenious economy. Better living was ahead, through research and
development, salesmanship and investment --- these were the tenets of
a secular religion, a salvationist faith in the signed papers and the head of
steam. Orders from major buyers, rockets to the moon, pistons pumping
and the whistle hooting! I leaned out the window and the wind hit me
full in the face.

'Twas in this thriving burg that I first got a hold on the world; and,
though my hold slipped loose, and the world I grasped was part illusion,
still I go back and pick at the seams and try to discover where the dream

slipped away. In my mind, Indians still crouch around campfires in the woods; Civil War armies, undersupplied, clash in the countryside; Tom Sawyer and Penrod Schofield run its byways; George Babbitt dreams at his desk downtown, patent medicine ads fill the papers, Elmer Gantry sets up his tent in a rented lot, sister Carrie boards the train for the big city, and tragic Prewitt, not yet in the Army, buys a pack of cigarettes at the roadhouse where Carl Perkins and his boys are tuning up.

For me, this was the romance of the country, and it set my head a-swirl. I was besotted.

Driving down the highway, now, from out-of-state, I switch on the radio and the local talkmeister tells me that my sort of person is working and hoping for America's destruction. His voice drips with fake knowingness. I ask myself, who licensed this copperhead to sink his fangs into me & mine and bring the hell of his hatred to earth and try to build a petty kingdom of it? Freedom of speech, they say? It sounds more like the freedom of the lynch mob. In the old days they used to whip them up about niggas and Catholics and Jews; nowadays it's the same old snake with a new set of fangs. Natural decency is the antidote to this poison; and I'm saddened that more people don't have it.

They want their country back? I want <u>my</u> country back!

Or did it ever exist, save in my youthful and exuberant imagination?